LIBRARY OF JAPANESE LITERATURE

The Golden Country

Boniface V. Lazzaro

December 1981

A Play by Shusaku Endo

THE

GOLDEN COUNTRY

Translated by Francis Mathy

Charles E. Tuttle Company

RUTLAND VERMONT & TOKYO JAPAN

Representatives
FOR CONTINENTAL EUROPE
Boxerbooks, Inc., Zurich
FOR THE BRITISH ISLES
Prentice-Hall International, Inc., London
FOR AUSTRALASIA
Paul Flesch & Co., Pty. Ltd., Melbourne
FOR CANADA
M.G. Hurtig Ltd., Edmonton

Published by the Charles E. Tuttle Company, Inc.
of Rutland, Vermont and Tokyo, Japan
with editorial offices at
Suido 1-chome, 2-6, Bunkyo-ku, Tokyo 112

TABLE OF CONTENTS

INTRODUCTION

In the hundred years between 1597, when twenty-six Christians were crucified on a hill overlooking Nagasaki, and 1697, when the last great martyrdom occurred in the province of Mino with at least thirty-five martyrs, no less than four thousand Christians are known to have given up their lives for their faith. In 1600 there were approximately three hundred thousand Christians in Japan. By 1700 Christianity had disappeared from the face of the nation and existed only in the small communities of hidden Christians that managed to preserve and hand down their religious traditions secretly until the return of the priests in 1865. Whatever caused the rulers of Japan to change from benevolent protectors of the foreign religion into its fanatical persecutors (fear of Portuguese and Spanish power seems to have been one of the main causes), this was one of the cruelest and most effective of the many persecutions Christianity has suffered in its two thousand year history.

From the beginning the persecutors were intent upon making apostates rather than martyrs. Since the ordinary death penalties by decapitation or crucifixion served but to win admiration for the martyrs, who went to their deaths joyfully, singing hymns and exhorting the crowds, crueler and crueler tortures were devised. To prolong the agony of victims at the stake, as well as to give additional time for reconsideration, wood was placed at some distance so that the sufferers roasted by the slow fire. Boiling water from the Japanese hot springs was slowly poured over the victims, a dipperful at a time. Christians were tied to stakes at the water's edge at ebb tide and slowly went to their deaths as the tide came in. Finally, the cruelest torture of all was devised—that of the pit. The victim's body and arms and legs were tightly tied with rope and he was suspended head first into a pit filled with offal. A hole was drilled in his temple to permit the blood to fall a drop at a time, thus preventing rapid death from circulatory obstruction. This torture could be made to last several days and even an entire week before death took place. It was extremely painful and very effective in inducing apostasy.

This is the historical backdrop of Shusaku Endo's play, *Ogon no kuni* (The Golden Country). *The Golden Country* was produced by the Kumo troupe under the direction of Hiroshi Akutagawa, son of the writer Ryunosuke Akutagawa, in the spring of 1966 and published in the May issue of the magazine *Bungei*. It has as its central character the Jesuit missionary Christopher Ferreira, who in 1633 after being tortured in the pit renounced his Christian faith, became an ally of the persecutors, and until his death by natural causes in 1650 worked with them in trying to make other Christians apostatize.

Christopher Ferreira was born near Lisbon, Portugal, in 1580. He entered the novitiate of the Society of Jesus at the age of sixteen. After six years of study for the priesthood, he arrived in Japan in 1602. Shortly afterward he went to Macao to complete his theological studies and was

ordained a priest there. Back in Japan he was assigned first
to the Kyoto mission and then to the one in Nagasaki.
From the beginning he caught the eye of superiors and was
marked for administrative office in the Society. In 1619 he
was named consultor to the Provincial, Father Mateo de
Couros.

From 1622 to 1626 he was Superior of the Jesuits in
Kyoto and seems to have performed this office with distinction. In 1632 he was made Provincial of Japan, and, there-
fore, Superior of all the Jesuits working in the country. The
annual report to Rome on the state of the mission was
written by him in 1628, 1629, 1630, and 1631; all are still
preserved in the Roman archives. The latter is especially
interesting since it gives a long, vivid account of the martyrs
at Unzen. In 1633 he was captured and tortured in the pit,
and subsequently apostatized. He was given the name of an
executed criminal, Sawano Chuan, together with his wife
and son, and he joined his former persecutors in their
inquisition.

In 1636 he wrote the book *Kengiroku* (A Clear Exposi-
tion of the False Doctrine), a closely reasoned attack on
Christianity. He also translated into Japanese a number of
Western works on medicine and astronomy. In later years
his name is found on a number of tribunals before which
the Christians were made to appear. For example, he was
on the tribunal in Edo in 1639 that condemned to death
the Japanese Jesuit, Father Kibe (of whom passing mention
is made in Act two, Scene two). Father Kibe in his final
moments zealously exhorted Ferreira to return to the
practice of his faith. But it was to no avail, for Ferreira
seems to have died unrepentant in 1650.

Why did he apostatize? The Ferreira of the play steps on
the picture of the face of Christ for one or more of the

following reasons. He believes that he has heard the voice of Christ urging him to stamp on the *fumi-e,* a plaque of Mary or Christ, or a crucifix, and thereby commits the act to save himself and the other Christians. Inoue, on the other hand, attributes his apostasy to the corroding influence of the "mudswamp" Japan, which causes all seeds from the outside to rot. In the final scene Inoue points out to Ferreira that his words are now more Buddhist than Christian and he concludes, "When it comes right down to it, it wasn't by me that you were vanquished but by this mudswamp called Japan."

Ferreira's action is open to still another interpretation, one that was particularly cogent in the Kumo production. Before turning himself over to his persecutors in order to save the Christians, Ferreira spends a night of anguish and pain, not unlike that of Christ in the garden of Gethsemane. When he finally overcomes his temptations and gathers together the courage to go to the Bureau of Investigation, knowing all along that it is undoubtedly a trap, Ferreira reaches a height of nobility and saintliness that makes everything that follows anticlimactic. The impression is given that the Ferreira who apostatizes is a man who has been broken and is no longer capable of free human action. This impression is reinforced by Inoue's boast to him:

> Through the torture of the pit, by tomorrow you'll have lost all discretion and understanding. You'll have lost your freedom to oppose my words. What I call left, you will call left. What I call right, you will call right. When I say "Apostatize," you will apostatize.

The Christians who witness the shameful act of their beloved pastor assume that he has gone mad.

Endo is more charitable in his interpretation of

Ferreira's defection than the facts seem to warrant. In the first place there were at the time of his capture and torture no farmers in prison or under threat of death for him to protect. This is a figment of the playwright's imagination. There were instead with him in the pit three other Jesuit priests (an Italian, a Portuguese, and a Japanese), a Spanish Dominican priest, and two Jesuit seminarians and one Dominican, the last three all Japanese. These endured the torture of the pit until death, which came after two, four, or six days. Ferreira, on the other hand, apostatized after only five hours. In the case of other priests who apostatized under torture there is evidence of later retractions, and all were made to spend the rest of their lives in prison, showing how little their captors could trust them. Ferreira is the only known case of a priest who apostatized, was set free by his persecutors, and then worked devotedly for their cause. The true reason of his defection must perhaps forever remain a mystery.

From the above it can be seen that the person of Christopher Ferreira has much to attract and challenge the novelist or dramatist. There are in his life all the elements of tragedy. Consecrated from an early age to the service of his God and the spread of his religion, he braved many hardships to take up life as a missionary in Japan. He must have had no illusions about the dangers of his assignment, since he arrived in Japan well after the persecutions had begun and several of his fellow Jesuits had already received the martyrs' crown. An energetic missionary and capable administrator, he was from the first highly regarded by his superiors and confreres and singled out for the highest offices a Jesuit could hold in the mission. His letters to Rome, especially his vivid account of the faith and courage of the martyrs, inspired a younger generation of Jesuits and filled them with the desire to join him in his perilous but glorious work. Yet after only five hours in the pit his character underwent a one hundred eighty degree change, so that the Dutch diarist at Dejima could comment that this former man of God "now goes about dirty and disheveled and has a black heart." Ferreira's book against Christianity is filled with hatred and the desire for vengeance. He is certainly a most dramatic figure in one of the most dramatic episodes of Japanese history.

Endo, as we can gather from the changes he has introduced in the story, is not simply interested in presenting the historical facts. He has fashioned his material into a problem play, revolving around themes that have already been sounded in his earlier works from the novel *Kiiroi hito* (The Yellow Man) in 1956 to the novel *Chinmoku* (Silence) published shortly before *The Golden Country*. *Silence* also is a tale of martyrdom and apostasy in seventeenth-century Japan, a companion piece to the play.

We have space here to touch upon only the principal theme, the disparity between Eastern and Western culture. The man from the East, in Endo's mind, can never really come to terms with the West. Tanaka, for example, the hero of the 1965 novel *Nanji mo mata* (And You Too) is completely broken in his attempt to understand and assimilate Western culture as a foreign student in Paris, and the gloomy conclusion of the novel is that the blood that produced the two cultures of East and West was of altogether different type. "We are unable to receive a blood transfusion from a donor of a blood type different from our own." On the opposite side, Father Duran, the fallen priest of *The Yellow Man*, who has left his priesthood to marry a Japanese woman, makes the same discovery. He finds in the Oriental's eyes "a lack of reaction, a lack of

emotion . . . [they are] eyes which are imperceptive of God
or sin, eyes which are unmoved by the thought of death."

In an early essay, *Christianity and I*, Endo states that in
some form or other Christianity is still the center of Western culture, even where it is attacked or neglected. But in
Japan there is no Christian history, tradition, sensibility, or
cultural heritage. "Even further," he continues, "there is
something in the Japanese sensibility that cannot accept the
Christian view. From my youth I began to discover this
puzzling Japanese sensibility in my environment and even
in myself." Endo goes on to specify this "puzzling Japanese
sensibility" as a threefold insensitivity not to be found in
the Westerner: an insensitivity to God (so that the very
question of the existence or nonexistence of God does not
even present itself to the Japanese), an insensitivity to sin,
and an insensitivity to death. He points out the difficulty of
making Christians of a people like the Japanese, who hate
extreme ways of thinking about evil and sin and who are
indifferent to the question of God.

In *The Golden Country* it is Inoue that expresses these
sentiments. Inoue is a relatively complex character. At one
time a Christian, he gave up his Christianity when he came
to believe that it was unsuited and unadaptable to Japan.
Still even as he persecutes the Christians and seeks to
eradicate the religion from the land, he holds on to the
hope that he may after all be mistaken. In Act two, Scene
two, Inoue tells Tomonaga that he rejected Christianity
when he came to see that the teachings of Christ could
never take root in Japanese soil, and he explains:

It isn't that the Christian shoots are bad in themselves.
Nor is this country of Japan bad. . . . But when a certain
plant will not grow in a certain soil, no matter what

means are used, then even the most stupid of farmers will know enough to either change the soil or pull up the plants. But the soil is this Japan of ours. There's no way of changing it. That being the case, there is no choice but to pull up the plants.

When Tomonaga protests that the plants were growing nicely until the persecution began, Inoue answers that they only seemed to be growing, they only seemed to be blossoming, and he adds:

Sometimes I get to dislike this country of ours. Or, more than dislike, to fear it. It's a mudswamp much more frightening than what the Christians call the devil—this Japan. No matter what shoots one tries to transplant here from another country, they all wither and die, or else bear a flower and fruit that only resemble the real ones.

To what extent does Endo identify himself with these sentiments? He is himself a practicing Christian, but, according to his own admission, one who experiences an interior conflict between his Christian self and his Japanese self. In a magazine interview he has stated that he received baptism when still a child. His Catholicism seemed like a ready-made suit and he had to decide either to make this suit fit him or get rid of it and find another.

There were many times when I felt I wanted to get rid of my Catholicism, but I was finally unable to do so. It is not just that I did not throw it off, but that I was unable to do so. The reason for this must be that it had become a part of me after all. . . . Still, there was always that feeling in my heart that it was something borrowed, and I began to wonder what that other self was like. This I think is the "mudswamp" Japanese in me. From the time I first began to write novels even to the present day, this confrontation of my Catholic self with the self that lies underneath has, like an idiot's constant refrain, echoed and reechoed in my work. I felt I had to find some way to reconcile the two.

The action of *The Golden Country* is centered upon the tension between Christianity and the "mudswamp," a tension that exists first of all within Endo himself. In the novel, *Silence,* it is the mudswamp that wins out. Not so in the play, which was written shortly afterward. The impression that caps the play and remains longest with the play-goer is that of the courage, nobility, and love of the martyrs. Against this concrete image, the abstract thesis of Inoue is powerless. Both the novel and the play, however, underline sharply the work that is still to be done in shaping essential Christianity into a form that will touch the strings of the Japanese heart and release his love and action. A Christianity that remains an abstract creed or a list of juridical prescriptions, of dos and don'ts, will never survive in the mudswamp. However this is not basically a problem of East and West, but of all human motivation, regardless of culture. Until the Christian apprehends the face of Christ as clearly and concretely as Gennosuke, the young samurai, apprehends the face of his beloved Yuki, it will be possible to go on stepping on that face. But Endo is right in saying that even after stepping on it, a start is at least made by continuing to look upon it with longing and loving eyes, as the fallen Ferreira does in the last scene of the play.

CAST OF CHARACTERS

Officials of the Bureau of Investigation of the Christians:
INOUE CHIKUGO-NO-KAMI   *in charge of the bureau*
HIRATA SHUZEN   *second in charge*
KANO GENNOSUKE   *a young samurai in the employ of the bureau*
FOUR OFFICIALS

Christians:
FATHER CHRISTOPHER FERREIRA   *Portuguese Jesuit Missionary priest in hiding*
TOMONAGA SAKUEMON   *landowner of the village*
YUKI   *his daughter*
HATSU   *a woman of the village*
KASUKE ⎫
MOKICHI ⎪
HISAICHI ⎬   *village farmers*
NOROSAKU ⎭
TOME   *apprentice to a candlemaker*
FIVE FARMERS

TIME: 1633
PLACE: Nagasaki

[16]

ACT ONE SCENE ONE

The scene is the Bureau of Investigation of the Christians set up by Inoue Chikugo-no-kami. Outside can be heard the voices of children singing the songs of the Buddhist festival of O-Bon.

INOUE: The night of O-Bon. The children's songs have a melancholy air. We've been in Nagasaki four months already.

HIRATA *(in a flattering tone of voice):* A very fruitful four months! Since your arrival the proscription of Christianity has been enforced from Nagasaki to Omura and Hirado, and most of the farmers have given up the foreign religion. Here in Nagasaki alone we've caught ten priests, five Japanese lay brothers, and seven catechists. My heartiest congratulations!

INOUE: But there's still much to be done. There are still priests in hiding. We capture the Christians one after the other. We force them to renounce their faith. The Christian entrusts himself to his strength of spirit. We assail his flesh. We test to see which is stronger, spirit or flesh. . . . But I'm tired of watching people. Don't you also find this work distasteful, Hirata?

HIRATA: No. Watching people is my duty. As an official, I must suspect everyone I meet. That is the only way to find out what others really are.

INOUE: The only way to find out what others really are! The Christians propose another way. You've got to trust people, they say. Only then do you find out what they really are.

HIRATA: But supposing there were a Christian spy planted here in the bureau. To all appearances one of us, energetically working with us; but in reality an ally of the Fathers and the Christian farmers. . . . You see, one cannot trust appearances. To smell out the reality, it takes someone like me.

INOUE: Then you would carry suspicion even to your fellow workers, even into the bureau itself. . . . I was once a believer in the Christian teachings, you know. That was when I was a retainer of Lord Gamo. So you must suspect even me. But do you mean to say that there is in fact a Christian here among us?

HIRATA: I didn't say that. I was only giving an example.

INOUE: An example? You're very crafty with your implications. . . . This Christian you speak of—is he someone close to me?

HIRATA: I leave that to your own observation.

> *Inoue drinks his tea, deep in thought. The sound of falling sand in the hourglass. The voices of the singing children are heard outside.*

INOUE *(lifting his head):* But do you have any proof?

HIRATA: What kind of proof do you want?

> *Inoue shakes his head and points his finger at Hirata. Kano Gennosuke enters.*

GENNOSUKE: Sir, Omura Ietada, one of the head samurai of the Omura clan, is here to see you.

INOUE: Fine. Show him into the study.

GENNOSUKE: Yes, sir.

INOUE: Gennosuke, just a moment.

GENNOSUKE: Did you call me, sir?

INOUE: Gennosuke, how old are you?

GENNOSUKE: I'm twenty, sir.

INOUE: You're not married yet, are you?

GENNOSUKE: No, sir. I've been too busy with my work to think of marriage.

INOUE: On the contrary, if you think so much of your job, you ought to find a good wife as soon as possible. Don't you agree, Hirata?

HIRATA: You're quite right, sir.

INOUE: Fine, you may go.

> *Gennosuke exits.*

INOUE: Hirata, I'll hear what you have to say later. But if there is really a Christian here among us, it will go very hard with him.

HIRATA: I haven't said anything about this to anyone else. I'll follow your directions. Perhaps before we pass the word on to Edo, we might make some private investigations of our own.

*Inoue exits. Hirata looks about him, then
signals to someone offstage. A guard
enters.*

HIRATA: Has the woman come yet? What was her name—
Tome?

GUARD: Yes, she's here.

HIRATA: Fine. When I give you the signal, bring her in.
But only when I signal, mind you.

*Guard exits. Gennosuke enters to clear
away the tea things from which Inoue
had been drinking. He sees Hirata and
greets him.*

HIRATA: Twenty years old, you say.

GENNOSUKE: Excuse me?

HIRATA: You said twenty, didn't you? That's a fine age to
be.

GENNOSUKE: Do you think so?

HIRATA: I was twenty once. Like you, I'd just entered the
bureau. I still knew how to trust people. But as I was
just telling Inoue, fifteen years of suspecting and
examining people have had their effect. The grime of the
job has seeped into my soul, habit has become nature.
And now I'm as you find me. Gennosuke, you'll be like
me someday.

He laughs.

GENNOSUKE: I don't want to be like you.

HIRATA: Everyone feels that way in his youth. But it's not
so easy. It's not so easy.

He pauses.

HIRATA: But to change the subject, I believe Inoue has been urging you to find yourself a wife.

GENNOSUKE: Yes, he's been so kind as to suggest this.

HIRATA *(sarcastically)*: Yes, of course. He's very solicitous, even for the young.

GENNOSUKE: Yes. I appreciate it.

HIRATA: What kind of bride will you look for?

GENNOSUKE: What?

HIRATA: I asked you what kind of bride you wanted. Are you too embarrassed to answer?

GENNOSUKE: I've never thought about it.

HIRATA: That's a lie. There's no youth of twenty that doesn't spend most of his time dreaming of the girl he'll possess.

GENNOSUKE: I'm not that kind of man.

HIRATA: Is that so? Then close your eyes. Even as we're speaking, the woman you'll spend your life with is somewhere to be found. Perhaps even here in Nagasaki.

GENNOSUKE: You're making fun of me.

HIRATA: Not at all. I'm not making fun of you. When I was twenty, that's all I thought about too. This girl who will be your wife—isn't she already in your heart? I can even guess what she is doing at this very moment.

GENNOSUKE *(led on by Hirata)*: What is she doing at this moment?

HIRATA: She's taking a crap. No, no, forgive me. I'm foulmouthed. When one gets to be my age, one falls into the habit of soiling beautiful things. I'm foul. Don't you agree?

He laughs.

HIRATA: But, seriously, tell me, what kind of girl do you want?

GENNOSUKE: My mother and I are all alone. I would like a good-natured wife that will be good to my mother.

HIRATA: A very proper answer indeed. This manner of speaking should get you far in the world. Do you mean to say that as long as she's good-natured, it doesn't matter to you if she's pretty or not?

Gennosuke mutters something inaudible.

HIRATA: I can't hear you.

GENNOSUKE: If she's pretty, it's all the better.

HIRATA: Then why didn't you say so in the first place? Do you have any notion why one of the head samurai of the Omura clan is here today?

GENNOSUKE: Not the slightest. Do you know why he's here?

HIRATA: Of course I do. These eyes see through everything that goes on at the bureau. This nose smells out everything that men try to hide. Otherwise I could never get the better of the crafty Christians. Just a moment ago you expressed some very lofty sentiments. But I have a clear picture of what's really in your heart.

GENNOSUKE: There's nothing there to embarrass me were it known.

HIRATA: I wonder.

He sniffs around Gennosuke.

HIRATA: You have a smell. You have a smell.

GENNOSUKE: You're carrying your game a little too far.

HIRATA *(as if speaking to himself):* No, the smell is all mine! Even I was once as young as you and reached out to the stars and dreamed great dreams. I can recall a winter morning when I walked aimlessly along the streets of Nagasaki and Maruyama, enraptured by the falling snow that purified the world about me. And an autumn sunset when I stood on Shian Bridge and sighed again and again the name of the girl I loved—which, incidentally, was the same name as the one you hold so tenderly in your heart, Yuki. What's the matter? When I mentioned her name, your face turned as red as autumn leaves.

> *Gennosuke hurries offstage as if in flight.*
> *Tomonaga Sakuemon enters.*

TOMONAGA: As usual, hard at work, I suppose.

HIRATA: Oh, it's you. I was just reminiscing with Gennosuke. I was telling him about the days long ago when I'd just entered the bureau. I guess that's a certain sign of age—when you start talking to the young about the past.

> *He laughs.*

HIRATA: I'm not so young any more.

TOMONAGA: You still have a long way to go. I'm the one that's getting old. And the work too has gradually become unpleasant. I've just returned from Hirado where I tried to settle a dispute between the Dutch and the English traders. Since there is something to be said for both sides, I came to consult Inoue.

HIRATA: Men have come in their ships across vast oceans to this far end of the earth. Men from the southern barbarian nations of Portugal and Spain, men from the northern barbarian countries of England and Holland.

They have come to us in pursuit of a vision, in search of a golden country. It occurs to me that our country is something like a man of good fortune chased after by a number of women. All four ladies, Spain, Portugal, England, and Holland, are energetically in pursuit.

TOMONAGA: Ho, ho. That's not a bad comparison. Of all these women, which will Japan take to wife? Which would you take to wife?

> *During the above conversation Inoue has entered and has been silently watching Tomonaga.*

HIRATA *(seeing Inoue, but pretending not to):* If I were a Christian, I'd have to follow the law of one husband-one wife. So I'd have to do as you urge—choose one from the four. But since I've never been a Christian, there's no need to make a choice.

TOMONAGA: No need to make a choice?

HIRATA: I'll make love to all of them.

TOMONAGA *(laughing):* No, no, my friend. If you wish to lead a life that is in any way human, you can't very well make love to a number of women at the same time.

HIRATA *(sarcastically):* Hear, hear! You're very strait-laced aren't you? A human life, you say? You must know, I'm sure, that a long time ago several daimyo of Kyushu who wanted Portuguese and Spanish trade gave up the whole project when they heard from the Fathers that a man wasn't permitted to keep another woman besides his legal wife. The Fathers must have told them what you're telling me now.

INOUE: Hirata, Hirata. Tomonaga Sakuemon is of quite a different stamp from you. He is a true samurai, who after death separated him from his wife never remarried but has remained continent to this day. Tomonaga, I'm afraid your work in Hirado has been fatiguing.

> *Tomonaga is flustered and turning to Inoue, greets him.*

TOMONAGA: I've just now returned.

INOUE: But, Tomonaga, there is something after all to what Hirata says. I also feel, as Hirata has put it, that our country is like a man set upon by four females. But to my mind, all of the four are nothing but harlots. People often speak of the whore with the heart of gold, as if only a whore really knew how to love. All the same, if one is chased by a pack of gold-hearted whores, there is no reason to pick one of them to be his wife. Long ago when I was a retainer in the Gamo clan, Lord Gamo maintained four households in addition to that of his legal wife. But his four concubines were extremely jealous of one another, and were constantly quarreling among themselves. So what do you think he did? He kicked all four out of his castle. The four barbarian nations, Spain and Portugal, England and Holland, have come to Japan obsessed by the dream of finding here a golden country. It seems to me that they are exactly like the four concubines I mentioned. They are jealous of one another and always backbiting. To Japan the unwanted attentions of these whores are a troublesome nuisance. That's what I think.

HIRATA: In that case, will you follow the example of the Lord of Gamo and throw all four out of the castle?

INOUE: No. I should say that that too would show lack of foresight. The concubines that were thrown out revealed to Nobunaga the inner affairs of the Gamo clan, and this was one of the causes for its downfall. But, Tomonaga, tell me the news from Hirado.

TOMONAGA: I agree with what you've just said. The traders from England and Holland are quarreling among themselves and making all kinds of accusations against one another. I've just returned here troubled.

INOUE: You shouldn't be troubled, you should rejoice. Just as at a horsemarket, the price of a horse goes up when there's more than one bidder.

TOMONAGA: You're right. I hadn't thought of that.

INOUE: We'll have ample time to hear your report later on. But just now there's something weightier on my mind. Hirata has just made a most startling statement.

HIRATA: Sir, it was not a statement—just a conjecture.

INOUE: You may have meant it as a mere conjecture, but when it is implied that there may be someone in the employ of the bureau—whether it be Hirata himself or Gennosuke or anyone else—someone here that still secretly follows the Christian teachings, then, conjecture or not . . .

TOMONAGA: Did Hirata really imply this? Everyone knows how zealous Hirata is in his work. I think that this implication too is a product of his zeal. But *(laughing)* it's hardly possible that an official here at the bureau could secretly be a Christian.

INOUE: That's what I think too. But, as I believe you well know, long ago I also was a Christian. So was Uchida Shuba. Ishii Hikojiro also was taught by Christians in his youth. Unless I am mistaken, Tomonaga, you too received baptism while Omura Sumitada was still alive. So you too have a guilty conscience.

He laughs.

INOUE: No, Hirata's so-called conjecture cannot simply be dismissed.

TOMONAGA: Please be reassured. You may have been a
Christian long ago, but you are now the chief official in
charge of investigating the Christians. And as for Uchida
and Ishii, wasn't it precisely because they'd once been
Christians that you brought them into the bureau?

INOUE: It's as you say. Both Uchida and Ishii, having been
Christians in their youth, best understand the movement
of the Christian heart. They know where the Christian is
weak and where he is strong, what kind of lies he will
tell to his interrogator, how best to press him. A
Christian who has given up his faith knows best how to
make another give up his. So Uchida and Ishii are both
of use to me.

TOMONAGA: Yes, that's true.

INOUE: It's the same with you. You are useful to us
because you gave up your faith. You are able to see
through the Christians' thinking. Isn't that so?

TOMONAGA: When you put it that way, I feel very much
as if I were one of the objects of Hirata's suspicion.

INOUE: Don't be ridiculous. I don't quite know how to
put it, but you are quite a different sort from Hirata.
Why, you even blushed at Hirata's little example of the
women. You're not the kind of man to conceal craftily
his true self and act out a part. Isn't that true, Hirata?

HIRATA: Quite true. If I even so much as suspected that
Lord Tomonaga was a Christian, I'd have to change my
whole method of investigating the Christians.

INOUE: And you, Hirata, must not be overzealous in your
work, to the point of losing perspective. By the way,
Tomonaga, do you happen to have heard of a priest by
the name of Ferreira?

TOMONAGA: Ferreira? Why, of course. Everyone's heard
of Ferreira. He's hiding out somewhere in Japan and
carrying on his work undetected by us. He's a Portuguese Jesuit, isn't he? I know that he came to this
country in 1600 and for twenty-five years has been
Superior of the Jesuits.

INOUE: You have quite a detailed knowledge of him.

HIRATA: He certainly ought to have. You see, when he
was still a retainer of the Omuras, he was one of those
baptized by Ferreira. Tomonaga, please don't take this
amiss. I have the custom of investigating thoroughly
those who are working for the bureau. I know too that
when you were a retainer of the Gamos, you let the
Fathers use your house as a church.

INOUE: You seem to have been born to distrust people.

TOMONAGA: No, no, it's as he says. Ferreira is a mistake
of my youth. I listened to his talks and even let him give
me the Christian name of Joseph. I'm very much
ashamed of this.

INOUE: Don't trouble yourself about it. I have a Christian
name too—Paul. There were many Johns and Pauls in
those days.

HIRATA: Besides, the mistakes of one's youth are hardly
to be avoided. But when even someone like Tomonaga
can go so far astray as to become a Christian, someone
like me . . .

TOMONAGA: Oh, is it possible that even someone like you
could go astray?

HIRATA: Of course it's possible. I once went so far astray
as to fall in love with a girl of the Maruyama pleasure
quarters named Yuki. Oh, forgive me. I had forgotten
that your own daughter is named Yuki. I always seem to

say the wrong things. I've heard that your daughter is eighteen years old. The young men working here with us told me. The man who gets her will be very lucky.

TOMONAGA: She's still only a child.

INOUE: You too will have a blessed future for having such a daughter.

TOMONAGA: Thank you for saying so, but she's only an ignorant country girl.

INOUE: You must be tired after your journey from Hirado. Take a good rest.

> *Tomonaga Sakuemon bows and leaves the room.*

HIRATA: You once told me, didn't you, that if you see a man with a totally unsuspicious face clapping his hands before the Buddha, he should be suspected of being a Christian. The same with a man pretending to be a fool. Or one who purposely makes fun of Christianity before others. All these, you said, are to be suspected of being Christians.

INOUE: I believe I did say that.

HIRATA: But what if such a man should seem most respected on the surface? Then what should one do about his suspicions?

INOUE: Conjecture is not proof. It's no laughing matter to arrest a samurai on mere conjecture. Don't let your zeal walk away with your head.

HIRATA: Excuse me. But I've got to catch Ferreira!

> *He claps his hands.*
> *Tome comes onstage, accompanied by the guard.*

HIRATA: Sir, please listen to what she has to say.

To Tome

HIRATA: Where do you work?

TOME: At a candle shop in Higashimiza-cho.

HIRATA: Someone has been buying a large quantity of candles at your shop each month this year, hasn't he?

TOME: Yes.

HIRATA: Please look at this receipt.

> *Hirata takes a paper out of Tome's hands and gives it to Inoue.*

HIRATA: Do you see whose name is on it?

INOUE: Tomonaga Sakuemon.

HIRATA: Why should he be ordering so many candles each month?

INOUE: For the Christian Mass, do you suppose?

HIRATA: He would hardly have use for this many candles in his home.

INOUE: Yes, I see.

HIRATA: And if these are for Mass, then a priest must be at hand. Could it be Ferreira? But even if it is not Ferreira . . .

> *Silence. Through the gate the children's singing can be heard.*

HIRATA: What shall we do?

INOUE: Throw suspicion on a man. Capture him, torture him, make him talk, spill his blood! . . . Oh, I'm sick of all this.

He comes back to himself, remains silent,
thinking, with eyes cast down.

HIRATA: Didn't you just ask Gennosuke if he weren't ready to find himself a wife?

INOUE: Yes. Tomonaga's daughter is not yet betrothed?

HIRATA: I don't believe so. Gennosuke seems to be in love with her from long ago.

After a pause, he continues, as if to
himself.

HIRATA: A Christian will marry no one but another Christian. Isn't that so?

INOUE: That's exactly what I was thinking.

Tomonaga has entered and is hidden in
the shadow. Inoue, looking in his direc-
tion, laughs.

CURTAIN

ACT ONE SCENE TWO

A month later. The scene is Korimura, a village on the outskirts of Nagasaki. A large barn used by the Christians as a meeting place. In the center is a large door. There is the sound of tapping at the door, one long and two short.

KASUKE: Kyrie eleison.

VOICE OUTSIDE: Christe eleison.

KASUKE *(opening the door):* It's Hatsu, with Mokichi and Hisaichi. Are you sure you weren't followed?

HISAICHI: We were having dinner when Mokichi came to say that Lord Tomonaga wanted to see us. I left everything and came on the run across the fields.

KASUKE: Have you heard the news? They've caught Brother Caspar in Nagasaki. And in Isahaya the officials walked in on a catechist and six Christians as they were saying their prayers.

Thinking for a while

KASUKE: It'll be our turn next.

MOKICHI: Enough of that talk! It's bad luck. That'll never happen here!

KASUKE: When I wake up in the middle of the night and think about it, I shudder. If even they who were hidden so well . . .

HISAICHI: If we're caught, we're caught.

NOROSAKU: If we're caught, we're caught.

KASUKE: This is no laughing matter. You're young and speak bravely. But what will you do if you're caught and brought before the bureau?

HISAICHI: I won't know until the time comes.

NOROSAKU: Won't know when the time comes.

KASUKE: Will you stand or will you fall? When they ask you "Do you give up Christ?" will you say "Yes, I give him up," or won't you? That's something you'd better start thinking about now. I suppose most people of the village will refuse at first to give in. In that case, what will the officials do next? You saw Moritaro of Isahaya when they sent him back after he'd given in. He was skin and bones, and black and blue all over. And that even though he'd done what they'd asked.

HISAICHI: I'll escape as long as I can. I'll hide from them as best as I can. And if I'm caught, whatever happens, I'll bear up under it as well as I can.

MOKICHI: What will you do, Kasuke? If they put you to the water torture or the fire, what will you do?

KASUKE: Me? There's nothing I can do but cling to God.

MOKICHI: Hatsu, you haven't said anything. What about you? Will you give in?

HATSU: God will never let such a terrible thing happen to

us. Didn't Father Ferreira tell us that he was merciful? He said that before things ever came to such a pass God would surely come to our aid.

MOKICHI: I also lived in that hope at first. But will God really come to our aid?

NOROSAKU *(in a loud voice):* He will come to our aid.

MOKICHI: I wasn't asking you, fool. Kasuke, Father said that those who gave up their lives would go to Paradise, didn't he?

KASUKE: Yes, he did.

MOKICHI: And that those who didn't bear up under the torture, and said "I give in" would go to hell?

NOROSAKU *(in a loud voice):* No, they won't go to hell.

KASUKE: Be quiet. If afterward they don't return to the practice of their religion but remain fallen away for the rest of their lives, they have betrayed God and are marked for hell.

MOKICHI: But here's the point! If we'd been born in a different age—not the present time of persecution but in the old days when everyone was Christian, including the daimyo, then we wouldn't have had to put up with all this. We'd have worked and prayed as Father told us, and would have peacefully made our way to Paradise.

KASUKE: What you say is true.

MOKICHI: A moment ago you mentioned Moritaro, who gave up his faith under torture. Now if he'd been born a generation ago, he'd probably have been a good Christian and gone to heaven. The other Christians would never have had cause to denounce him as a traitor worthy of hell. It was just his bad luck to have been born in this age of persecution. He couldn't stand up under the torture, and so he fell. The more I think about it, the less I understand.

As if angry

MOKICHI: That's the way I look at it.

NOROSAKU: That's the way I look at it too. I can't understand.

HATSU: Mokichi, what are you saying? You mustn't murmur against God's Providence.

NOROSAKU: That's what I think too. You mustn't murmur against God.

KASUKE: He may be somewhat thick, but life is certainly easy for him—no worries, no problems.

HATSU: Father says that it was for his own good that God didn't give Norosaku more brains than he needed.

HISAICHI: Norosaku, what do you think Paradise is like?

NOROSAKU: When I enter the gates of Paradise, Santa Maria will greet me. Then she will wait on me until I've eaten my fill. And then she'll offer me saké and I'll drink it down.

MOKICHI: That's enough. It's easy to see why he's a Christian.

The sound of tapping on the door—according to the prearranged signal.

MOKICHI: Kyrie eleison.

VOICE OUTSIDE: Christe eleison.

Five or six Christians of both sexes enter.

WOMAN: We came in the rain.

All are shaking out their wet clothes. The sound of rain grows louder.

KASUKE: It's too bad we have to post a guard on a night like this, but Heizo, please keep a lookout for us. If you see or hear anything suspicious, give the signal.

> *Heizo opens the door to leave. Father Ferreira, Lord Tomonaga, and Yuki are standing at the door.*

TOMONAGA: Kasuke, did you post anyone on guard?

KASUKE: Yes, Heizo was just going out.

TOMONAGA: It's dangerous tonight with just one man. Please send another with him.

> *At Kasuke's signal, one of the farmers goes out.*

TOMONAGA: The reason I called you all together this evening is this. The chief investigator, Inoue Chikugo-no-kami, has decided to make a final effort to pull out all the roots of Christianity. He intends to go from village to village, wherever there may be hidden Christians, and make each farmer step on the *fumi-e.*

KASUKE: What's a *fumi-e?*

TOMONAGA: A *fumi-e* is a plaque of Mary or Christ, or a crucifix. He'll try to make us step on it.

KASUKE: Step on it?

TOMONAGA: Yes, in front of the officials he will order us to step on the face of Christ or Mary. Those who do so at once will be released. Those who don't . . . Unless they will sign a pledge of apostasy . . .

> *He turns his eyes downward.*

TOMONAGA: Sooner or later—no, very soon, they will bring the *fumi-e* here too. I came to tell you so you wouldn't be caught unawares.

MOKICHI: But even knowing it beforehand . . . there's no escaping it, is there? What did we ever do to deserve this? Why must we spend each day in such fear? I don't understand. We've never neglected to pay our yearly tax of rice or make our annual work contribution, even the women and children. All we've done is live according to the religion our fathers and grandfathers went to so much trouble to pass on to us. Is it for this that we must receive such treatment?

TOMONAGA: I know without your telling me what you're going through. And because I know it, I've hurried to bring you this message.

MOKICHI: Sir, what would you do in our place? . . . If you were asked to step on the *fumi-e*?

TOMONAGA: What would I do?

He laughs.

TOMONAGA: Five years ago when Otomo Kazen gave up the faith he'd received from his father, and ordered all his retainers to do the same, I also signed the pledge of apostasy. I didn't want to do it, but finally did—for three reasons. The first, of course, was just sheer weakness. But, secondly, I wanted to be of some help to Father Ferreira, and I wanted to be able to give my protection to you, to all my people. And so I became an official of the Bureau of Investigation and have so far succeeded in escaping detection. But I've made up my mind that I must one day declare publicly what I am. For that reason, should Inoue bid me step on the cross or on the face of Christ, I'm determined to give witness to my faith, whatever pain may be inflicted on me. But I am a samurai and you are farmers. I should never blame you for stepping on the *fumi-e*.

MOKICHI: Father says that those who give up their faith go to hell.

TOMONAGA: That I don't know. All I know is this: those who give up their lives for Christ will on that very day pass through the gates of Paradise. I know that Santa Maria will bind their wounds and that Jesus will wipe away their tears. That I know.

HISAICHI *(with force):* I'll never step on it. I'll never step on it.

NOROSAKU: I'll drink saké with Santa Maria in Paradise.

TOMONAGA: But frankly, Hisaichi, I think you ought to consider seriously whether it might not be better to step on the *fumi-e* after all. However shameful, you'd at least remain alive. As a samurai, I can't do that. But you can. You'd remain alive to pass on the teaching of Christ secretly to your children and grandchildren. Then the Christian faith would keep a foothold in this country. That's one way of looking at it.

HATSU: I'll never step on it. No matter what happens. This life is painful enough for us farmers. Born farmers, farmers we remain to the end. We're already in the fields each morning before the moon has hidden itself from view, and we're still at work after the sun has set. We plant the rice knee-deep in cold water, and when it ripens and is harvested we must give it away to pay our tax. We're called out on public duty and must go even if we are sick. In the pain of daily living we've fixed our hearts on the joys of Paradise. And if after all this we are unable to reach Paradise, but giving up our faith must face the tortures of hell, then we are worse off than animals. I can't bear to think of it.

> *The other farmers listen intently to Hatsu's words.*

TOMONAGA: Well, at least tonight there's no *fumi-e* to worry about. Think it over carefully and decide what stand you will take. But I have something else to tell you. Inoue intends to plant a dog in your midst.

KASUKE: A dog?

TOMONAGA: Pretending to be a Christian, he'll walk among you and report everything he sees and hears to the bureau.

All are disturbed.

TOMONAGA: No, he's not here yet. But be on your guard. . . . Who wants to confess his sins and his doubts to Father and receive the grace of the sacrament? I'll go first. Wait outside, but take good care that you're not seen.

The farmers open the door and go out into the rain.

TOMONAGA *(keeping his eyes fixed on the door, says to Yuki):* You too had better go out and prepare for confession.

She exits.

TOMONAGA: Why is God silent? Why doesn't he help us? Even if he doesn't help me, why does he allow these poor farmers to be cornered like this? These five years Christians everywhere have been captured and tortured, and a tremendous amount of blood has been spilt. Why does he remain silent through all this? In Hirado, in Omura, in Isahaya, in Nagasaki, so much blood has flowed!

FERREIRA *(as if to reassure himself as well):* Do you think these trials are meaningless? Do you think that God would send us suffering just for its own sake? Lord Tomonaga—

He shakes his head vigorously

FERREIRA: The Lord would never send us such meaningless tribulations.

TOMONAGA: Then what is it? Why does he send them,
Father? You know these Japanese farmers. In their
ignorance they have followed along like children.
Plunged into the boiling waters of Unzen, they held on,
believing that this was the way to Paradise. Even when
they had huge rocks tied to them and were dropped into
the middle of the sea, with their last breath they sang
out their prayers. . . . This is true fealty. Even as a
samurai, I have never to this day seen so great a fealty.

FERREIRA: And the Lord rewards such fealty with great
glory.

TOMONAGA: I also try to explain it this way. For these
five years I have believed this. Even now I still believe it
in my heart. But occasionally when I am disheartened, I
am attacked by doubt. I wonder if these are not just
words to keep our eyes from the truth.

FERREIRA: What do you doubt?

TOMONAGA: What need is there for such a vast stream of
blood to continue to flow? When I see the farmers
stricken with such fear and lamentation, I wonder if God
has not deserted us.

FERREIRA: Whatever God does is good.

> *Ferreira walks to the other side of the
> room, picks up a bundle in a corner, and
> draws out of it a painting of Christ.*

FERREIRA: Lord Tomonaga, look at this face of Christ. It
is probably the Christ of the Sermon on the Mount.
Have you ever wondered what Christ looked like? No
one knows what his face was really like. Nowhere in the
Scriptures is a description of it. But this face . . . it is a
face that men through the centuries have formed in their

prayer born of suffering and trials. Take a good look at it. Can this beautiful face be indifferent to our cries? Can it pretend not to see our suffering?

TOMONAGA: Don't try to put me off with beautiful words. Tell me the truth, Father. Isn't God keeping a cold silence? Isn't he silent in spite of the suffering of these farmers?

FERREIRA *(weakly):* In these trials God is trying to tell us something.

TOMONAGA: What?

FERREIRA *(painfully):* That I don't know. But you must at least believe that he is trying to get something across to us.

TOMONAGA: Father, as I told you before, Inoue and the other officials have begun to suspect me. No, it's even more than this. They've found something out about me. The other day Inoue made the proposal that Yuki marry a young samurai by the name of Gennosuke who is employed at the bureau.

FERREIRA: It's a trap, isn't it? He knows that if you are a Christian you will not consent to your daughter's marrying one of the persecutors of the Christians. He's waiting to see what you'll do.

TOMONAGA: Of course it's a trap. At the time, I was able to put him off, but sooner or later he will come up with another test. As I told the farmers, my mind is set. As a samurai, it is only proper that I give up my life for my God. But they are weak farmers. It's for their sakes that I ask you to clear up quickly the doubts I mentioned to you. Please give an answer to my question. Why does God remain silent? Why doesn't he speak in spite of all this suffering of the Christians? . . . No, I mustn't talk in this way.

Yuki enters with a white veil on her head.

YUKI: Have you finished? I'm ready for confession.

TOMONAGA: Yuki, make a careful confession. Confess
your smallest sins and doubts. So that you may be
washed as white as snow. Don't be ashamed of anything.
It's painful to confess one's weakness, but this very pain
cleanses the soul. Do you understand?

YUKI: Yes, I understand.

> *Tomonaga bows to Ferreira, then exits.*
> *Ferreira sits to hear Yuki's confession.*

FERREIRA *(reciting the opening formula in Latin):* Be
brave. Go ahead and confess.

> *Yuki remains silent.*

FERREIRA: Have you done anything to stain your soul
with sin?

YUKI: Father, a girl like me . . .

> *She falls into silence again.*

FERREIRA: A girl like you . . . yes?

YUKI: A girl like me . . . No.

> *She starts again.*

YUKI: Will God forgive a person for being in love?

FERREIRA: By being in love do you mean a husband
loving his wife, or a girl like you falling in love with
some young man? No, no, that's not a sin. Not at all. Far
from being a sin, God made man and woman in such a
way that they would fall in love with each other. Just as
in spring the trees burst into fragrant flower and birds
begin to sing, so this too is blessed by God. And didn't
Christ help to celebrate the wedding feast at Cana?

YUKI: And will he also give his blessing if the man is not a Christian, but, what's more, a member of the bureau persecuting the Christians?

FERREIRA: A member of the Bureau of Investigation? Yuki, that man wouldn't be the young samurai who works for the bureau, would it? That couldn't be, could it? Why don't you speak? Can't you hear me? Speak out.

YUKI: Yes, it's Gennosuke.

FERREIRA: I was right. . . . Since when have you known him?

YUKI: Since I was a child. We used to play together. At times when the older children wouldn't let me enter their games and I stood crying, he would take me by the hand and sing songs to me. Since then I've always looked upon him as a brother.

FERREIRA: You needn't go into detail about the past. Did you meet him occasionally after that?

YUKI: No, I never met him again until I heard about him from my father the other day. But . . .

FERREIRA: But? . . . Continue.

YUKI: I've been all flustered since father told me about the proposal.

FERREIRA: Are you in love with him? . . . Remember, he's an official. No, official would be bad enough, but young as he is, he is an official of the bureau in charge of the Christian persecution.

YUKI: That's the very reason why I am suffering.

FERREIRA (silent for a moment): I know how much you are suffering, Yuki. My heart goes out to you. But as a priest, I must tell you clearly: you must stop thinking about him. You must get over this infatuation. From this day on you must look upon the suffering you ex-

perience in erasing him from your heart as the cross
which Our Lord himself places on your shoulder. And
you must carry it just as Christ carried his heavy cross,
that was laid on his shoulders that day in Jerusalem. You
must bear patiently the pain of giving him up. It won't
be easy, Yuki. It will be torture. But Our Lord knows
you are experiencing this pain.

YUKI: Yes.

FERREIRA: You must pray to him with all your heart.

> *The priest gives her absolution in Latin.*
> *Yuki leaves. Ferreira stands up. The*
> *sound of a door opening.*

FERREIRA: Who is it?

KASUKE: It's me, Father—Kasuke.

FERREIRA: And the others?

KASUKE: We've put our heads together and have tried to
come up with a plan, but no good one comes to mind.
Sooner or later the officials will surely come to our
village too. There's no way to escape. Father, when that
time comes, will Jesus and Santa Maria help us? If Jesus
knows everything, why won't he save us? . . . No, that's
not what I wanted to say. The bonze at the infidels'
temple has been running around the streets telling everyone that the Christians' God cannot save his people from
torture by fire and water. Why does he disturb people
with his stupid chatter? If I catch him, I'll beat him over
the head. That's what I've told myself.

FERREIRA: You promised to beat him up?

KASUKE: Yes, that's what I promised myself. . . . Listen,
Father. When we farmers plant our crops, we have good
seedlings and we have bad. With the good ones, all we
have to do is plant them and they thrive. But the bad

ones—no matter how much fertilizer we heap over them, they refuse to grow or to bear fruit.

FERREIRA: What does this have to do with what we were talking about?

KASUKE: Father, among the Christians too—no, even among the farmers in this village, there are the good seeds and the bad, the strong and the weak. This has nothing to do with their piety. Those born with a strong heart are able to bear up under torture; they are able to persevere in their piety. But those born weak and cowards—no matter how set they are to suffer torture, their shaking bodies won't listen to their hearts.

Growing more excited.

KASUKE: Soon our village will also have to meet the test of the *fumi-e*. Father, you won't be able to help us then; each of us will be on his own. The strong among us will be able to put up with any pain the officials may inflict. They will never step on the face of Christ. But those of us who have been born weak cowards—what about us?

FERREIRA: God will certainly help you in that moment. Why do you doubt it?

KASUKE: Father, I've heard these words so often. But will Jesus really help the weak as well as the strong? Then why did he himself throw the weak shoots into the river? Those without strength? I'm talking about the really weak—those that won't grow no matter how much fertilizer is used, or how tenderly they are cared for.

FERREIRA: What weak shoots did Christ throw into the river? What are you referring to?

KASUKE: You yourself told us about that. I'm speaking of the coward that betrayed him.

FERREIRA: You mean Judas?

KASUKE: Yes, Judas. Won't you tell me about him once more? Then I can make clear to you what I mean.

FERREIRA: The night before he died on the cross, Jesus ate a last supper with his twelve apostles. It was evening and all were seated in their places, taking their meal. Then Jesus spoke: "One of you will betray me," and dipping a piece of bread into a dish, he handed it to Judas, saying "Be quick on your errand."

KASUKE: That's it. When you told us that story, I couldn't understand it. Christ is full of love for men, isn't he? Then why didn't he show love to a coward like Judas too? Christ knows everything. So he must have been able to look into the coward Judas' deepest heart. And he was willing to see him fall into hell without helping him or trying to stop him. In other words, he will let us put our feet on the *fumi-e;* he will let us deny our faith. He will desert us before everyone's eyes. Isn't that true, Father? He pulled out the weak shoots and threw them into the river. That's what it looks like to me.

FERREIRA *(strongly):* Kasuke, do you think that Our Lord rejected Judas in anger and in hatred?

KASUKE: Forgive me, Father, but that's what it looks like to me.

FERREIRA: Listen carefully. There was once a farmer whose wife had deserted him, wasn't there? I forget his name. Do you suppose that when he threw her out it was for sheer hate? Not at all. He was still in love with her, and just because he was in love with her, it was very painful for him to look upon his traitorous wife. He must have been torn in two directions—on the one hand, by his still-burning love for his wife, and, on the other, by his hatred for her act of betrayal. And so he told the woman: get out of my sight. Consider what was in that man's heart, Kasuke. Our Lord's feeling toward Judas must have been similar.

KASUKE: Father, please don't get angry. I was just concerned about the fate of the weak seedling.

FERREIRA: But, Kasuke, Christ can transform that weak seedling into a strong one.

KASUKE: How, Father?

FERREIRA: Through the power of prayer. That's what you are forgetting. Just believe. When your heart is clouded with doubt, pray—with all your strength. Please think over what I've said.

Kasuke exits.

FERREIRA *(facing the painting of Christ):* Lord, if Lord Tomonaga's plea and Kasuke's words have reached you, please make an answer. I can no longer encourage them with my own words. Even though my lips frame a reply to their doubts, my heart no longer assents. I am suffering from the same anguish and doubt as those farmers. Why do you remain silent? You are always still. I know that one word from you would change everything. If you would only respond to our suffering, we would be strengthened. Why must we face pain and torture by fire and water? Is it impossible for us to believe in you while we are in a condition of happiness? Why is it bad to be happy? Why do you permit your people to fall and then continue to afflict them? Please tell me. Please speak to me. Why do you remain silent?

Staggering

FERREIRA: The silence of the night—only the stars are alive. The earth is cold. Is my faith also weak? Am I tempting you with my cries? I'm gradually falling into the sin of hypocrisy.

CURTAIN

ACT TWO SCENE ONE

It is the following afternoon, the same scene as Act one, Scene two. Hatsu and Yuki are mending Mass vestments, a red and a black.

YUKI: Hatsu, this is the vestment used in the Mass for the Dead. Black stands for the sorrow of those left behind. The red vestment is worn in the Mass of the Saints who gave up their lives for Christ. Father told me that the red is for the precious blood of the martyrs.

HATSU: Yes?

YUKI: Hatsu, did Father bring these vestments across the far seas with him?

HATSU: No, they were given to him by a great Father who died in Japan. Now only these two are left. With sun, wind, and rain, the colors have faded.... Yuki, Father told me that even when he was running from place to place like a dog, trying to keep ahead of the officials— even then he kept these two vestments with him always, along with his breviary.

YUKI: Father came to this country the year I was born, didn't he?

HATSU: He was here in Nagasaki and made many trips to Yamaguchi and Kyoto. But even this distance, he used to say, was nothing compared to the dangerous journey to Japan from his native land.

YUKI: Hatsu, won't you put that vestment on for a second?

HATSU: This vestment? But it's the vestment Father uses to say Mass.

YUKI: Only for a second. No one will ever know.

HATSU *(putting it on):* Like this?

YUKI: Oh, it looks very nice on you.

HATSU: Nice on *me?* Please don't tease me.

YUKI: I would like to see that vestment, not as it is now, faded and worn, but as it once was, a flaming crimson, burning like the evening sun of Nagasaki that dyes the seas red. I would like to attend a Mass as in the old days, when all sang out in a loud voice, and the altar was buried in flowers, and among the flowers a shining gold crucifix.

She falls silent.

HATSU: Is something wrong, Yuki?

YUKI: No, nothing. Nothing.

She covers her face with her hands and sobs in a low voice.

HATSU: How strange you are! A moment ago you were joking and had me put on the Mass vestment, and now you're weeping. I must say, I can't understand you young girls.

She shakes her head.

YUKI: But you're not so old yourself.

HATSU: Why did you suddenly burst into tears?

YUKI: You wouldn't understand.

HATSU: Yuki, don't make fun of me. If I knew what was wrong, I wouldn't ask. Come on, tell me.

YUKI: Do you promise not to tell anyone?

HATSU: I promise. May I go to the inferno if I am lying.

> *Hatsu and Yuki turn their backs to the audience and speak together in a low voice.*

HATSU: So you refused to marry Gennosuke, the young samurai. I know how you feel. But I'm sure he doesn't hold it against you. You're probably more upset about it than he is.

YUKI: But what must he think of me?

HATSU: He belongs to the bureau, a young samurai hunting for Christians. It doesn't matter much what he thinks, even if he is hurt or dies. . . . No, no, that's not a Christian way of talking. Even if he is one of our persecutors, we must be kind to him. Are you in love with him, Yuki? I can't know unless you tell me. Speak out.

YUKI: Yes, I love him.

HATSU: Ah, is that so? You're just at the right age. I see how you feel about him. Fine, then. I'll see to it that he finds out your true feelings.

YUKI: But how?

HATSU: I have a cousin named Tome who works at a candle shop in Nagasaki. She sometimes delivers candles to the bureau. I can have her tell Gennosuke secretly of your love.

YUKI: No, no, you mustn't. Then all of my father's pains till now would be to no avail. Everyone at the bureau would find out that we're Christians.

HATSU: Oh, I wouldn't have Tome tell Gennosuke that you're Christians! She'd only say that you love him but have a very good reason for refusing to marry him.

YUKI: I wonder if it would work. No I'm sure it wouldn't. In the first place, how do we know that we can trust Tome? Besides, to do such a thing without first con- sulting my father. . . . Still, if we could do it in such a way that he wouldn't find out. . . .No, no, I'm sure it wouldn't work.

> *The door opens and Kasuke, Mokichi, and Norosaku enter.*

HATSU: What do you mean by bursting in here without giving the signal?

KASUKE: There's no time for such things. Where's Father Ferreira?

HATSU: In the shed in the back. He's writing something. But what's the matter? Why are you so excited?

MOKICHI: They brought the *fumi-e* to the village of Miwa yesterday.

HATSU: And what happened?

KASUKE: Those who wouldn't step on it were led away to the bureau in Nagasaki.

MOKICHI: All along the way the officials beat them with whips and sticks, as if they were horses or cows. The women and children who fell were kicked brutally.

KASUKE: At their head stood the apostate, Moritaro. He's the one who told the bureau about the Christians of Miwa. But he'd had a change of heart, and was with the Christians in the procession, weeping and wailing.

MOKICHI: The apostates become the tools of the bureau as it tries to get even one more Christian to give up his faith. Just as the devil will do everything in his power to swell his ranks by even one, so these fallen Christians work to drag others into their evil.

HATSU: Stop that fearful talk in Yuki's presence.

KASUKE *(to Yuki):* Forgive me. I thought it best to tell Father Ferreira about this.

> *Kasuke and Mokichi quickly exit to the rear.*

NOROSAKU: Why is everybody making such a fuss?

HATSU: It's nothing. In a short time many of the Fathers will come to Nagasaki from across the distant seas.

NOROSAKU: With the sign of Jesus on their sails.

HATSU: That's right. You remember that song very well, don't you?

NOROSAKU: I remember. Shall I sing it for you?

> *He sings.*

NOROSAKU: *The Pope's ship approaches these shores*
With the sign of Jesus on its sails.
Now it can be seen approaching
The Pope's ship with the sign of Jesus on its sails.

HATSU: Well done. Someday, Norosaku, you'll be able to go out to meet the Pope's ship, coming straight from the country called Rome, on its sails the name of Mary. And there'll be many Fathers aboard.

NOROSAKU: On that day I'll greet the Fathers. Then they'll ask me, "Norosaku, will you have something to eat?" and I'll answer, "I will." And they'll ask me again, "Norosaku, would you like to have some saké to drink?" and I'll answer, "I would."

HATSU: That's right.

Kasuke, Mokichi, and Ferreira enter.

KASUKE, MOKICHI: Good-by Father.

They exit.

HATSU *(looking steadily at Ferreira):* What will happen to us? ... No, no, nothing will happen. I was just telling Norosaku that in a short time we'd all go out to welcome the Pope's ship bringing over many new Fathers.

FERREIRA: Yes, yes. There's nothing to worry about. The Lord will see that everything works out for the best.

NOROSAKU: And that ship will take us to the temple of Paradise.
We're on our way, we're on our way,
We're on our way to the temple of Paradise.
The temple of Paradise is far away,
The temple of Paradise is far away,
But we're on our way, we're on our way,
We're on our way to the temple of Paradise.

Father, what kind of place is Paradise?

FERREIRA *(gently):* Paradise, Norosaku? It's a place where all of the present sadness and pain will have completely disappeared, where we'll enjoy ourselves completely with God.

NOROSAKU: Then I'll be able to eat as much as I like, won't I? All the millet and dried fish I can eat. And Santa Maria will serve me.

FERREIRA: Yes, Santa Maria will gladly serve you. It's a place where gentleness of heart will overflow like golden light. Like spring in my native Portugal.

YUKI: Father, tell us about your country.

NOROSAKU *(with emphasis):* In your country, Father, can everybody eat until they're filled?

FERREIRA: My country? My country is Japan. I came across the far seas to become a Japanese. I'll never return again to Portugal. It's now just the country where my past is buried. Still, when I close my eyes like this, I see before me the white walls of the city. In spring the windows are all bright with red roses and the sun sparkles on the sea. When the noon Angelus drifts quietly between the rows of houses, the young girls come to a halt and make the sign of the cross.

YUKI: Father, tell us how you left your country and came to Japan.

FERREIRA: It took me four years to get here. I first passed along the southern coast of the hot continent called Africa. It was two years before I reached Goa in India. Many times the ship had to stop at neighboring ports because of storms or epidemics, or for lack of water. Many of the sailors died in the course of the journey. It took another year to get to Macao, and still another from Macao to Japan. Finally I reached the port of Hirado.

YUKI: Father, why did you leave your native land? I've heard that you left behind a mother and sister.

FERREIRA: I came because I had a dream of Japan as the golden country. I didn't dream of buried gold as did the Portuguese merchants. No, no, rather I think of Japan as the golden country where the teachings of Christ can really take root.

YUKI: It seems to me, Father, that it is your country that is the golden country.

FERREIRA: Distant objects always seem beautiful. What is beyond reach always attracts. That is why one's memories are always beautiful.

NOROSAKU: That's true. That's true.

YUKI *(as if dreaming):* What is beyond reach always attracts! Maybe that's why he seems so attractive.

HATSU *(trying to cover up for Yuki's slip):* Are you speaking of Christ?

YUKI: I wonder if he holds it against me.

HATSU: Why should Christ hold anything against you?

NOROSAKU: Yes, yes.

FERREIRA: Now please leave me alone for a time. Yuki, Norosaku, there's nothing to worry about. Norosaku can dream about the meal that awaits him and Yuki can imagine the country I left behind. And so you will spend the day pleasantly.

> *Yuki, Hatsu, and Norosaku leave the room.*

FERREIRA *(bringing out the painting of Christ):* Lord, how long must I go on with this painful pretense? Why must these innocent ones suffer tomorrow under the whips of the persecutors? In spite of all, your face remains so silent and unperturbed. Too silent, too unperturbed. At the river of boiling water, in the death-colored streets of India, I tried to come at least one step closer to your face. But at this moment what I want to see is not your serene face, but your suffering face—your face lined with fear and disfigured with sweat and blood. "And now Christ was in an agony and prayed still more earnestly; his sweat fell to the ground like thick drops of blood."

> *With the painting of Christ in his hands, he walks staggeringly offstage.*
> *The sound of a creaking door, Hatsu silently enters.*

HATSU *(looking about):* Norosaku.

> *Norosaku follows her onstage.*

HATSU: Do you understand, Norosaku? You want to eat your fill, don't you? You want to have enough millet and dried fish, don't you?

NOROSAKU: Father said I should spend the day thinking about what I'd eat.

HATSU: Then, Norosaku, listen carefully to what I tell you. I can't bear to see Yuki's tear-stained face. Can you go to Nagasaki by yourself?

NOROSAKU: I'll go. I'll go.

HATSU: You know my cousin Tome who works in the candle shop, don't you? Will you go to her and tell her that I've a favor to ask of her and that she should meet me secretly at Ienontsuji. Don't forget the place—Ienontsuji. Do you have it? You want to eat your fill of millet and dried fish, don't you?

CURTAIN

ACT TWO SCENE TWO

*The scene is the Bureau of Investigation.
It is evening. Tomonaga Sakuemon is
sitting alone. Gennosuke enters.*

GENNOSUKE: Please wait a moment, sir. Inoue-dono will
be in shortly.

TOMONAGA: He sent word that he had something special
to talk over with me. You don't happen to know what it
is, do you?

GENNOSUKE: No, I have no idea.

TOMONAGA *(pointing to an hourglass):* That's a most
unusual piece, isn't it?

GENNOSUKE: It's an hourglass given to Inoue-dono by the
Dutch traders in Dejima.

Gennosuke bows and prepares to retire.

TOMONAGA: Gennosuke.

GENNOSUKE: Yes.

TOMONAGA: You've really made good.

GENNOSUKE: Thank you, sir. But why do you say this
now? You've been observing me all along.

TOMONAGA: The old days suddenly came to mind. Your
mother must be happy at your success.

GENNOSUKE: You've all helped me to achieve it.

TOMONAGA: Gennosuke, success is very important for a
samurai. But there is something else of importance—
virtue. Just as a woman, a samurai too must have a
virtuous heart. Don't forget that.

GENNOSUKE: No, sir, I won't.

> *Gennosuke retires. Tomonaga sits with
> his eyes fixed on the floor, deep in
> thought. Hirata enters from the garden.*

HIRATA: Oh, it's you.

TOMONAGA: Hirata-dono.

HIRATA: Have you seen Inoue yet?

TOMONAGA: No. What does he want to see me about?

HIRATA *(feigning ignorance):* Could it be about your
daughter again?

> *Gennosuke, who has just entered with
> tea, perks up his ears.*

TOMONAGA: But we declined the proposal on the last
occasion.

HIRATA: This is a different matter. . . . She's as pretty as a
flower. No wonder that Lord Omura is taken with her.

TOMONAGA: Lord Omura?

HIRATA: What, haven't you heard?

TOMONAGA: I've heard nothing.

HIRATA: Then I shouldn't be telling you this since Inoue hasn't said anything to you yet . . . but I'm very envious of you.

TOMONAGA: What's this all about?

HIRATA: Very well, I'll tell you. But promise not to let on to Inoue that I said anything. He'd be furious with me.

TOMONAGA: I promise.

HIRATA: You know, I think, that one of the chief samurai of the Omura clan, Omura Ietada, came here secretly the other day.

TOMONAGA: Yes. I was formerly a retainer of the Omuras, so I came to pay my respects.

HIRATA *(keeping Tomonaga in suspense):* That's a very unusual clock isn't it? It's an hourglass sent over by the Dutch traders.

TOMONAGA: Hirata . . .

HIRATA: One of the chief samurai of the clan came secretly to consult Inoue about Lord Omura Suminaga.

TOMONAGA: Is that so?

HIRATA: Lord Omura lost his first wife last year and is greatly disadvantaged without her. He asked Inoue to find someone to take her place.

TOMONAGA: You can't mean that Yuki . . .

HIRATA: Exactly. Inoue feels that you cannot be happy giving your daughter to a house of as low a rank as Gennosuke's and that you wouldn't decline to send her to Omura Castle, since you were once a retainer there. He spoke of this to me this morning.

TOMONAGA: I could never accept.

HIRATA: Why do you say that?

TOMONAGA: Yuki . . . is still a young girl. She could never fill such an important position.

HIRATA: Do you mean to say that you find it distasteful to send your daughter to the house of your former lord? Do you reject Inoue's plans?

TOMONAGA: To take care of Lord Omura, you say? In other words, to do him service in the night. Isn't that it? More properly called, a concubine. That's against the proper way of man and woman.

HIRATA: Aren't you somewhat exaggerating? What you're saying, then, as I understand it, is that unless your daughter becomes Omura's legal wife, you will not give her to him. You'd better consider your social standing.

> *Gennosuke, who has overheard the conversation, hurries out of the room.*

HIRATA: The way of man and woman, you say. This sounds like Christian talk to me.

TOMONAGA: Hirata.

> *Without reflection he lays his hand on his sword.*

TOMONAGA: What are you saying? Are you in your right mind?

> *Inoue enters, pretending not to see what is happening.*

INOUE: Is it you, Tomonaga? I'm sorry to have kept you waiting. Hirata, I've something personal to discuss with Tomonaga.

HIRATA: Excuse me.

> *He bows and leaves.*

INOUE: How are you?

TOMONAGA: The fact is that Hirata. . . . No, it's nothing.

INOUE *(looking closely at Tomonaga):* Are you sure?

TOMONAGA *(trying to change the subject):* Is this an hourglass?

INOUE: Yes. I received it from the Dutch tradesman, Luhmer. Is this the first time you've seen one?

TOMONAGA: No. I saw one once in Hirado.

INOUE: I have something still more interesting.

> *He brings out a telescope, a pistol, and other objects, and shows them to him.*

INOUE *(claps his hands, and Gennosuke appears):* Gennosuke, bring the cakes from Portugal.

GENNOSUKE: Yes, sir.

INOUE: This is a telescope. It's the best one I've ever had in my hands.

> *Tomonaga looks at it.*

INOUE: No, the other way. From that end everything looks smaller.

> *Gennosuke brings in tea and* castella.

INOUE: Gennosuke, what's wrong? Your hand is shaking.

> *Gennosuke doesn't answer.*

INOUE: *(laughing):* You may go. Today, strangely enough, everyone seems to be on edge. . . . This is what is called *castella.* Try it. Please help yourself.

> *Tomonaga pulls off the paper wrapper and takes a bite.*

TOMONAGA: So this is *castella.*

Inoue brings out a large painting of Christ.

TOMONAGA: Oh, are there still things like this around?

INOUE: This is a fine piece of work. It's a European painting which several generations of Christians in Yamaguchi have kept in secret. It's irreplaceable as far as they're concerned. The story is that Francis Xavier gave it to them as a keepsake when he left Japan. Take it in your hands. It's rather heavy.

Tomonaga takes it. Inoue keeps his eyes fixed on him.

INOUE: Isn't it heavy?

TOMONAGA: What did you say?

INOUE: I asked if it was heavy.

TOMONAGA: No, not in the least.

INOUE: Is that right? You were once a Christian. Isn't this Christ heavy to your hands and to your heart?

TOMONAGA: I've forgotten it long ago—that heaviness you mention.

INOUE: Of course, of course. Were it otherwise, you'd hardly be able to work here to persecute the Christians, would you?

TOMONAGA: You were also a Christian. And your knowledge of Christianity has stood you in good stead. You've been able to make the Christians reject their faith one by one. Until you came they'd been able to withstand all torture.

INOUE: But there are still priests at large that I haven't been able to catch. For instance, Father Kibe and Father Ferreira. But I'll get them too someday.

TOMONAGA *(in a challenging tone):* This is a matter of some importance to you, isn't it?

INOUE: Yes, it is. Of great importance.

He laughs.

INOUE: But tell me, Tomonaga, why did you throw over Christianity?

TOMONAGA: Would it have been better if I hadn't? If I hadn't done so, by now I'd have been called before the bureau and strictly examined by you.

He raises his voice in a laugh.

TOMONAGA: But what was your reason for rejecting Christianity?

INOUE: Why did I reject Christianity? Because I came to see that the teachings of Christ could never take root in Japanese soil.

TOMONAGA: It's hardly that they can't take root. Isn't it rather that since Hideyoshi's time we've been systematically uprooting them?

INOUE: Certainly it's as you say. Since Hideyoshi we've been uprooting whatever came to our attention. Even now I'm busy at that work. But I had a slightly different purpose.

TOMONAGA: Do you take pleasure in your work?

INOUE: I can't say that there isn't some pleasure in injuring a woman that one has madly loved. And I was once completely enraptured with the teaching of Christ. But I am not pulling out living shoots. It's because I do not think these shoots will thrive on Japanese soil that I uproot them.

TOMONAGA: You don't think that the teaching of Christ suits the Japanese soil?

INOUE: It isn't that the Christian shoots are bad in themselves. Nor is this country of Japan bad. That much even
I will agree to. But when a certain plant will not grow in
a certain soil, no matter what means are used, then even
the most stupid of farmers will know enough to either
change the soil or pull up the plants. But the soil is this
Japan of ours. There's no way of changing it. That being
the case, there is no choice but to pull up the plants.

TOMONAGA: But at one time the plants grew nicely.
There was a time when even in Japan there were as many
as two hundred thousand Christians, and churches were
standing not only here in Kyushu, but also in the
Chugoku and Kamigata areas.

INOUE: The plants were not growing. They only seemed to
be. They didn't blossom. They only seemed to do so.
Don't you see that? Sometimes I get to dislike this
country of ours. Or, more than dislike, to fear it. It's a
mudswamp much more frightening than what the
Christians call hell—this Japan. No matter what shoots
one tries to transplant here from another country, they
all wither and die, or else bear a flower and fruit that
only resemble the real ones.

TOMONAGA: This Japan was the dream country of the
East to the European priests and traders. They even
called it the golden country.

INOUE: The golden country? Its natives are more spirited
and intelligent than those of all other non-Christian
countries. Who was it that said that?

TOMONAGA: It was St. Francis Xavier.

INOUE: That was only a self-deluding dream, and they
tried to force this dream upon Japan. The golden
country? This mudswamp? They considered this sterile
land that can't support a single healthy shoot—they

considered this a fertile field? They tried to plant here
the shoots of God. But in this mudswamp called Japan
God's shoots would not grow. Long ago I also became a
convert to Christ. But I was little by little betrayed by
this mudswamp.... A moment ago, didn't you say *Saint*
Francis Xavier?

TOMONAGA: From old custom. It just slipped out.

INOUE: Words that just slip out generally manifest a
person's true feelings. Being in the employ of the
bureau, you must surely know that.... At least, that's
what Hirata would say. But what do you think of this
painting?

TOMONAGA: What shall I say? I don't want to be taken to
task for another slip of the tongue. Shall I say only that
it's a fine piece of work and leave it at that?

> *He laughs.*

INOUE: I wonder if Christ had a face like this.

TOMONAGA: I don't know. But all the paintings brought
over by the Fathers have this same kind of face.

INOUE: Long ago when I was a Christian, I once asked one
of the Fathers about the face of Christ. He told me that
even in the Scriptures there was nothing written about
it. In other words, this face must have been imagined by
those who came later.

TOMONAGA: I don't know.

INOUE: Yes, it must have been imagined. It's a face made
up of man's petitions, his griefs, his joys, his dreams over
a period of many years. Just as the face of Buddha is a
face made up of the poor farmers' fantasies, this face of
Christ embodies all the dreams of the Christians. To a
woman, it is the most beautiful masculine face; to a

man—just look. Such tranquillity, such strength, such reserve!

TOMONAGA: Is that so? Such a painting no longer has any meaning for me. It's like a gold coin to a cat. No matter what kind of face it is.

INOUE: What if we should ask the Christians to step on this face?

TOMONAGA: I don't understand.

INOUE: If we ask them to stamp on this picture with their feet?

Tomonaga looks down in silence.

INOUE: Is there any man that would step on the face of the woman he loved when told to do so? Not a one. Similarly, is there any Christian that would step on what is for him the most beautiful, the most precious face in the world?

TOMONAGA: But it's only a painting.

INOUE: Not at all. And because it is something more, I will make the Christians step on it. I have thought up this *fumi-e*. This is my revenge on those who don't realize that Japan is a mudswamp, or pretend to ignore the fact.

He laughs.

TOMONAGA: But it's only a painting. Even the Christians can distinguish between the real Christ and a painting of him. I think you underestimate their intelligence.

INOUE: No, that's not it. Even I, who have now renounced the Christian faith, would feel pain in stepping on this painting. Do you mean that you could step on it without feeling anything?

Tomonaga doesn't answer.

INOUE: It is only people like Hirata that could step on it and think nothing of it. What about you?

TOMONAGA: I think I could step on it without hesitation.

INOUE: Really? Then let's make a trial of it. Go ahead and step!

TOMONAGA: You want me to step on it? I gave up Christianity long ago. It should hardly be necessary for me to prove it to you. Besides, it wouldn't do to harm this painting.

He tries to change the subject.

TOMONAGA: By the way, just a minute ago Hirata mentioned something to me.

INOUE: Hirata? What did he say?

TOMONAGA: He spoke about my daughter.

INOUE: He can't keep anything to himself. Was it about the proposal from the Omuras?

TOMONAGA: Yes.

INOUE: The argument I overheard as I entered the room—was it about that?

TOMONAGA: Yes, forgive me.

INOUE: Don't worry about it. If you are against the match, I'll tell the Omuras myself.

TOMONAGA: Then please do. My daughter is just a young girl and could hardly fulfill such a function.

INOUE: There's just one problem, Tomonaga. Should you refuse this offer, unpleasant rumors will get started. That's what I'm worried about. You're a former retainer of Lord Omura. People will surely say that the only reason why despite your former connection with the

Omuras you refuse to give your daughter to them is that you are a Christian. That's not my opinion, you understand. That's not my opinion, but if there gets to be too much talk, it will be unpleasant for both of us.

TOMONAGA: Is there such a rumor circulating about me?

INOUE: I can't say that there isn't. It has even reached my ears. Sometimes there are even great exaggerations, such as that you are hiding Father Ferreira.

TOMONAGA *(laughing):* All talk without any foundation!

INOUE: Is that so? That may be, but I should like to have you prove clearly to the members of the bureau that you've indeed renounced Christianity.

He claps his hands.

GENNOSUKE: Did you call, sir?

INOUE: Please call Hirata-dono.

HIRATA *(enters with a guard):* I'm here.

INOUE: Hirata, if Tomonaga steps on this painting before your eyes, will you let go of your suspicions? He says he'll step on it. Tomonaga, please go ahead.

TOMONAGA: Why?

INOUE: For my sake. When you step on it, your legs will certainly hurt. My heart will also hurt. But the seed of Christianity will not grow in Japanese soil. Be aware of this.

HIRATA: How about it, Tomonaga? If you've really abandoned Christianity, then it won't be difficult for you to step on the painting. But even should he step on it, I wouldn't stop being suspicious.

He claps his hands. Tome enters.

HIRATA: Tome, tell us what happened the other day. What did the girl Hatsu tell you Yuki had said?

TOME: Yuki said that she was in love with Gennosuke. She hadn't wished to refuse his proposal of marriage, but there were unavoidable circumstances. That's what Hatsu said. I asked her again and again what those circumstances were. At first she didn't say anything.

HIRATA: At first she wouldn't tell you?

TOME: Then she told me. Yuki is a Christian.

Silence falls upon the group.

TOMONAGA: Yuki? It's not her fault. I knew that sometime this moment would come. Sooner or later it was bound to come to this. Inoue-dono, you said just now that the seed would not grow, in this mudswamp called Japan. But I, just like the Fathers, believe that Japan is the golden country.

INOUE: Then you won't step on the painting?

TOMONAGA: No, I won't.

He makes the sign of the cross before the painting.

TOMONAGA: I am a Christian.

HIRATA: Where is Ferreira hiding?

TOMONAGA: I don't know. What will you do to me?

INOUE *(sadly)*: Why did you have to be so foolish? Why did you have to admit that you were a Christian? Why do you have to die? Just because you die a martyr's death, this country of Japan will not change. A mudswamp is for all time a mudswamp.

TOMONAGA: If it's a mudswamp, then our deaths will be the fertilizer that will make it fruitful.

INOUE: Do you really believe that? I'm willing to make a wager. You may die today, I sometime later. After the passage of many years the Fathers may once again return to this country. But even then, I wager that what the Christians call the seed of God will not grow in this country. Hirata, take him away. Hang him in the pit . . . until he tells you where Ferreira is hiding.

HIRATA: Like a samurai, turn over your sword.

TOMONAGA: Like a samurai.

> *He turns over his sword, bows to Inoue, and follows the guard. Inoue has his eyes fixed on the floor.*

HIRATA: Now that Tomonaga has confessed, there should be no trouble in finding Ferreira. Won't you leave the rest to me?

INOUE: Hirata, life is very simple for you, isn't it? You live it at its lowest level, don't you?

HIRATA: What do you mean?

INOUE: Oh, nothing. I only meant to say that in every society men like you spread out as luxuriantly as weeds and prove to be quite as hardy. . . . I think I know how we can catch Ferreira. I'm not like you. I don't go after men for the joy of catching them.

> *In a low voice.*

INOUE: I've placed a wager.

HIRATA: Oh? What have you wagered?

INOUE: Am I right? Or are the Christians right? Is Japan really a golden country in which the seed will grow, as Tomonaga says; or is it a swamp, as I think, a swamp in which the roots rot and die. But you wouldn't understand. It's all right. Go ahead.

Hirata bows and retires.

INOUE *(seeing Gennosuke with eyes downcast):* Now there's a real samurai, this Tomonaga.

Gennosuke remains with eyes down.

INOUE: You must certainly hate me. Because I played with your heart in order to get Tomonaga to confess. I made light of a man's heart. But politics in every age is of this nature.

Gennosuke bows and retires.

INOUE: I'll catch Ferreira. But will he fall, or won't he? This is what I must find out—for my own sake. This is my wager. Through Ferreira, I torture myself.

CURTAIN

ACT TWO SCENE THREE

The scene is once again the Christians' meeting place in Korimura.

HATSU *(to Norosaku):* Norosaku, won't you sing the hymn "We're on our Way to Paradise" once more?

NOROSAKU: *We're on our way, we're on our way,*
We're on our way to the temple of Paradise.
The temple of Paradise is far away,
The temple of Paradise is far away.
We're on our way, we're on our way,
We're on our way to the temple of Paradise.

HATSU: That hymn was sung by a man named Jiroemon from the island of Goto. The inquisitors begged him again and again to give up his faith and they tortured him brutally. But he wouldn't give them the sign. And so they put him on a boat and headed for the island of Naka-enoshima in mid-ocean, planning to kill him there. And this is the hymn he sang on the boat.

NOROSAKU: And then they sent him to Paradise.

HATSU: There are no trees or shrubs on Naka-enoshima. It's a frightening island, with only bare rocks. They

[72]

made Jiroemon stand on top of the rocks and they urged him once more to give up his faith.

NOROSAKU: Then they sent him to Paradise.

Yuki and Kasuke enter.

KASUKE: Lord Tomonaga hasn't come back yet?

HATSU: No, not yet.

KASUKE: He went to the bureau yesterday and he's not back yet.

HATSU: Yuki, what shall we do?

YUKI: I want to see Father Ferreira.

Ferreira enters with Hisaichi.

FERREIRA: What's the matter?

KASUKE: Lord Tomonaga hasn't come back yet. He's been gone since yesterday.

FERREIRA: Did he leave any word?

YUKI: No.

FERREIRA: Don't worry. Sudden business may have come up.

NOROSAKU: And then the man standing on top of the cliff was sent to Paradise.

Sound of knocking at the door.

HISAICHI: Who is it?

MOKICHI: Mokichi.

Mokichi enters.

MOKICHI: Father, Father . . .

KASUKE: Not so loud. He's right over here.

MOKICHI: A young samurai has just come saying he has important business and must by all means speak to Yuki.

HATSU: Is he one of the officers of the bureau?

MOKICHI: He said she'd understand if I told her that Gennosuke had come. He says he has news of her father that he must pass on to her at once.

YUKI: I'll speak with him, Father.

FERREIRA *(leaves one candle lit on the altar, but extinguishes the rest):* It's best if you all return quietly with Yuki. Take care not to be seen. Hisaichi, stay at Yuki's side and don't leave her on any condition. Kasuke, please help me here.

> *Exit all except Ferreira and Kasuke, who conceal the altar.*

FERREIRA: What's the matter?

KASUKE: My tooth. I have a toothache.

FERREIRA: Look at this.

> *He shows him a crucifix, then continues as if speaking to himself.*

FERREIRA: Do you think that Christ didn't feel the same weakness of flesh as you? What about the Garden of Gethsemane? When he sweat blood. It was blood he sweat. Just as you and I, he must have struggled against a great fear.

KASUKE: Father, do you suppose that Lord Tomonaga's been caught? In that case, they'll be after us shortly.

FERREIRA: It's not yet certain.

KASUKE: I'll step on the *fumi-e*. I know it. I try to imagine myself taking your hand and the hands of the other Christians and going with you to Paradise, but my body refuses to follow such a dream. To tell the truth, Father, I'm scared. I'm scared of being tortured and I'm scared of dying.

FERREIRA: You're not the only one that's scared.

KASUKE: No. In this world there are the strong and the weak, just as there are girls with pretty faces and those with ugly. Those with pretty faces go through life attracting men, while the others lead lonely lives. This is just the same. The strong, like Tomekichi of Isahaya, are able to put up with any suffering; are never afraid, no matter what terrible experience they're made to undergo. He was taken into God's home. But in my case, though I want to go along with Tomekichi, this body is frozen with fear.

> *He falls to the ground and weeps. The door opens with a screech.*

FERREIRA: Who is it?

> *He sees Yuki standing there.*

FERREIRA: Yuki, what has happened?

YUKI: Father's been taken as we feared.

FERREIRA: Lord Tomonaga taken?

YUKI: Taken and is now hanging in the pit.

FERREIRA: Who told you this?

YUKI: Gennosuke came to tell me.

> *From the shadow of the door, Hatsu and Gennosuke enter.*

FERREIRA: Yuki, did you bring him here?

YUKI: Please forgive me, but there was no other way.

GENNOSUKE: Please forgive this intrusion. But don't

scold Yuki. I'm also a samurai. I'll never mention this to anyone.

FERREIRA: You're one of the officers of the bureau, aren't you?

GENNOSUKE: Yes, I am. But I did not come here in that capacity.

KASUKE: Father, you must not be deceived by that officer's words.

FERREIRA: Lord Tomonaga is now hanging in the pit, you say?

GENNOSUKE: Yes.

FERREIRA: And what is the pit?

GENNOSUKE: It's a torture devised by an official of the bureau named Hirata. A man is bound, a small hole is drilled in his temple for the blood to trickle out, and he is hung upside down in a deep pit.

YUKI: Ohhh.

HATSU *(supporting her):* Don't lose heart, Yuki. . . . It's my fault for placing so much trust in Tome.

FERREIRA: Is he being pressed to give up his faith?

GENNOSUKE: He's a samurai. He hasn't said a word to indicate that he'll give in.

FERREIRA: We knew that. He's a samurai of samurai. He pretended for a long time to have renounced his faith in order to shelter us.

GENNOSUKE: Inoue also knows that he'll never give in. The reason he continues to torture him . . .

FERREIRA: The reason he continues to torture him?

GENNOSUKE: He wants to find out where you are, Father.

YUKI: Ohhh.

GENNOSUKE: Inoue has told him that if he reveals your hiding place, he won't have to renounce his Christianity. He says that he'll even overlook Lord Tomonaga's practice of his faith as well as that of the farmers of the village. He's very cruel.

FERREIRA: In other words, if I fall into the bureau's hands, he promises to spare Lord Tomonaga's life.

GENNOSUKE: Yes. But Lord Tomonaga will never tell them.

> *Ferreira steps backward, the eyes of everyone on him.*

FERREIRA *(confused)*: Do they say that they'll let him go if they catch me? That's just their strategy. It's a trap. Why did you come here? You had no reason. Why did you come to tell us this?

GENNOSUKE: I came . . . I had several reasons. I came because Lord Tomonaga always had kind words for me. My mother brought me here once. From childhood I have wanted to be a samurai like him. And now he . . .

FERREIRA: That's just a pretext. You came here on Inoue's orders to draw me into a trap.

GENNOSUKE: Do you have so great a suspicion of me? Then I'll tell you. I didn't come just to tell you what happened. I came because I wanted to save the life of Lord Tomonaga, because I wanted to help Yuki.

FERREIRA: The bureau tried to arrange for your marriage to Yuki, to find out whether Lord Tomonaga would accept or refuse.

GENNOSUKE: That's your imagining. There was a proposal to give her to Lord Omura, but Lord Tomonaga, of course, refused point blank.

FERREIRA *(drawing back):* Lord Tomonaga is suffering
this moment for me. If I give myself up, he'll be released. Is that your story? But even after I'm caught, it's
a very simple matter for the men of the bureau to take
his life too.

GENNOSUKE: I must go back. Unless I do, it'll seem
strange.

KASUKE: When do they plan to bring the *fumi-e* to this
village?

GENNOSUKE: Oh yes, that's something else I had to tell
you. The day after tomorrow.

> *Kasuke gives a loud moan. Gennosuke*
> *bows to Yuki, then leaves. Yuki follows,*
> *calling after him,* "Gennosuke!" *Hatsu*
> *walks off with her.*

FERREIRA: It's a trap. What the young samurai said . . .
that's just their strategy. They're not so soft as to spare
Tomonaga's life just because they catch me. I know. I
know how crafty these Japanese officials are. It's
nothing but a trap.

KASUKE: Father, won't you please help the people of the
village?

> *He crawls to him on his knees.*

KASUKE: It's not just his life. Whether *we* live or die
depends on you alone. Please, I beg you like this with
folded hands. I'm afraid, I'm afraid.

> *The door opens and Hisaichi, Mokichi,*
> *and other villagers carry in Yuki, who has*
> *fainted.*

HATSU: Father, Yuki has fainted. . . . It's all my fault. I
did a terrible thing.

KASUKE: The bureau has Lord Tomonaga in the pit. The *fumi-e* will come to this village the day after tomorrow. Inoue promises that if Father gives himself up, Lord Tomonaga and all of us will be saved.

FERREIRA *(draws back, as all look intently at him):* Why do you look at me that way? Why do you look at me with those eyes?

He covers his eyes with one hand.

FERREIRA: Don't you understand that this is a trap the bureau has set for us? What reason do they have for letting you go? Listen. Do you really believe that they will free Lord Tomonaga if I go to take his place? Do you really believe that knowing you are Christians they'll pretend not to know? I can't follow that kind of reasoning. Listen. I'm the only priest left in Japan. As priest, I am for you the Church itself. When I'm gone, there'll be no one to give you absolution for your sins, to pour the saving waters of God upon your children. This is what I want you to consider.

All are silent.

FERREIRA: Don't look at me that way. Don't look at me with those eyes. What have I done to you? Lord, why do you make a victim out of me? I am not Christ. Why are you silent? O Lord!

All are frightened by Ferreira's expression and draw back.

FERREIRA: Leave me alone. Get out. Through that door.

All hurry to leave as if in flight.

FERREIRA *(falling to his knees):* O Lord. Lord, you can see to the very bottom of my soul. You know my weakness of spirit. Until now I have acted as a priest and handed on your teachings to these people. As if I were

really somebody. Standing on some kind of pedestal.
Just as if I were prepared to overcome any obstacle that
might come along. But now, I see myself as I am, this
miserable self. My ugly face. Is this the true self? Then
how does my faith differ from that of the coward? This
is something that never struck me until today. What does
it come to? I traveled across wide oceans to Japan, just
to labor for you, just to serve you as your servant. O
Lord, then you present me with this comedy.

He laughs.

FERREIRA: The Garden of Gethsemane. If even Christ
sweat blood, how can I endure alone? I can't. I can't.
Mary, my Mother, intercede for me. Intercede for me
that the strength will be granted.

> *The spotlight moves from Ferreira to
> another portion of the stage, where Yuki
> and Hatsu are praying in the same posture
> as Ferreira. Next to them stands
> Norosaku.*

YUKI: Mary, Mother Mary, intercede for us. Obtain for me
the strength I need. What shall I do?

HATSU: Can you forgive me? It was because of my foolish-
ness that your father was caught.

YUKI: Pray along with me. Hail Mary, full of grace, the
Lord is with thee. Blessed art thou amongst women. . . .
It's no use. The prayers to Mary which usually fall like
petals from my lips are now like tasteless grains of sand.
Even as I kneel here, my father is hanging upside down
in the pit. . . . Ohhh, I see him suffering before my eyes.

HATSU: It's the same with me. O Santa Maria, why do you
let this happen? I was just trying to help Yuki. Santa
Maria, why do you play with me like this? Whatever I
may have done, you must help the people of the village.

You must help Yuki's father, Santa Maria. Even if I did do it, it's not my fault. It's all your fault—for playing with us like this. Yuki, why don't you ask Gennosuke's help?

YUKI: He's a very kind person, but he promised the farmers not to say anything about Father Ferreira's hiding place. No matter how hard Gennosuke tries, father can't be saved unless Father Ferreira goes to the bureau.

HATSU: Yuki, ask Father Ferreira.

YUKI: Then my father's sufferings would come to an end. If that were possible, my anguish would be over.

NOROSAKU: And then that man was sent to Paradise.

The spotlight turns again to Ferreira.

FERREIRA: What do you wish of me, Lord? What do you order me to do, miserable as I am? If you tell me to sacrifice my life to save Tomonaga and the villagers, I will gladly go and give myself up. But then there'll be no shepherd left in this country to hand on your teaching. There'll be no priest to take your place and to confer on the people your living waters. I am the only remaining priest in this country. Do you wish this last light to be quenched? Please answer. O Lord, in this difficult time I can't decide what to do without your help. I'm now blind. So blind that I can't even see into myself. Lord, why are you silent? You are always silent.

A voice is heard laughing.

FERREIRA: What is that laugh?

He plugs his ears.

FERREIRA: What is that laugh.

The spotlight turns now to Kasuke and Hatsu.

KASUKE: What's Father doing?

HATSU: He's been closed up in his room for a long time. He doesn't come out.

KASUKE: So, after all . . .

HATSU: Kasuke, the day after tomorrow they bring the *fumi-e*.

KASUKE: Don't even speak about it.

HATSU: But if Father goes to the bureau, they'll pretend not to know about us. The man from the bureau said so.

KASUKE: We can hardly rely on their word. It's as Father said. The officials at the bureau are not the kind of men that keep their promises.

HATSU: But there's no other way of being saved than by trusting in their promises. Have you thought about that?

KASUKE: Ah, if only God would come to our help in such a time!

HATSU: Is there any possibility of that? If there were, then he would have been watching over the lives of the Christians long before. When Kiheie of Omura was taken, we prayed very hard, but Kiheie was burned to death all the same. When the mother of Jiro of Isahaya was taken, then too God simply folded his arms and looked the other way.

KASUKE: What are you trying to say?

HATSU: I'm just putting into words what all of you are thinking but are afraid to say. You, Kasuke, the day after tomorrow when the *fumi-e* comes . . . you'll lift your hands in prayer. But God won't hear you. He won't come to your help. You'll meet the same fate as Jiro's mother.

KASUKE: Why do you torture me like this?

HATSU: Listen, Kasuke. There's only one way to save the life of Lord Tomonaga and protect the people of the village.

KASUKE: What way?

HATSU: Won't you go with me to the bureau? We can offer to exchange information concerning Father's whereabouts for the life of Lord Tomonaga.

KASUKE: Those are terrible words.

HATSU: Then you place but little value on your life. Do you want to hang upside down in the pit like Lord Tomonaga?

> *The spotlight shifts back to Ferreira. He still hears a voice laughing.*

FERREIRA: Who's laughing? Am I deceiving myself? Is that your meaning? That laugh! Is it laughing at me? Yes, it's true. I've been telling lies to myself. And not only to myself. I've been lying also to you, Lord. The truth is that I'm frightened. I'm afraid of being killed. That's why I won't go to the bureau. That's why I won't go even to help Tomonaga and the farmers. I've taught many people how glorious it is to die a martyr's death and yet when I'm pushed to it, I tremble with fear like this. How foul, how foul. O Lord, if it be your will, let this cup pass from me, but not my will but thine be done. "And now Christ was in agony and prayed still more earnestly; his sweat fell to the ground like thick drops of blood."

CURTAIN

ACT THREE SCENE ONE

> *The same scene as Act one, Scene one,*
> *Inoue's Bureau of Investigation. A*
> *painting of Christ hangs on the wall.*

HIRATA: I wonder if Christ really looked like that.

INOUE: No. According to the Fathers, there's nothing written anywhere about how Christ looked.

> *He takes up another painting of Christ.*

INOUE: This was painted by the Italian Giovanni Niccolo, who came to Nagasaki in 1585.

HIRATA: I've only heard the name. He must be the one who introduced the Japanese artists to European painting.

> *He inspects it.*

HIRATA: But this Christ has the same face as the other. And these were all painted from imagination!

INOUE: Not just imagination. If there is any face that artists beyond the seas have conceived out of their dreams and longings, it is this face. They painted it as the most beautiful of all human faces and the most precious.

> *Gennosuke enters with tea. Inoue stares at him.*

HIRATA: But it's still all imagination. I can only believe what I see.

INOUE: Gennosuke, your hand is shaking.

GENNOSUKE: It's nothing.

> *The clock strikes. Far off a wailing voice is heard.*

INOUE: What's the matter, Gennosuke? Are you frightened by Tomonaga's wails?

GENNOSUKE: I can't bear to hear them.

INOUE: He's a brave man. He's been hanging there for almost a day, but he won't give in. And he won't tell us where Ferreira is hiding. He's a samurai among samurai. His kind are rare these days.

> *Gennosuke hurries out of the room. Inoue and Hirata silently drink their tea. Occasionally Tomonaga's cries break the silence.*

INOUE *(as if to himself):* Torture. Inflict pain. Shed blood. . . . I'm sick of all this.

HIRATA: What did you say?

INOUE: Nothing. . . . What are you thinking of?

HIRATA: I was just looking at this painting . . . at this face that you call the most beautiful and most precious.

INOUE: Yes?

HIRATA: Man's a very strange creature. When he hears that it's the most beautiful face, he feels an urge to defile it. When he hears that it's the most precious face, he wants to spit on it. When I look at this painting, I am filled with such desires.

INOUE: Have you ever had any unpleasant experiences?

HIRATA: No, never. I know I'm foul.

He laughs, but suddenly stops.

HIRATA: Who's that?

TOME: It's me. I came to tell you that a farmer of the village has something to say to you.

HIRATA: Is that right? The plan's going very well indeed.

He lowers his voice and speaks to Inoue.

HIRATA: Everything is working out according to your scheme.

INOUE: I knew it would . . . from the moment I saw Gennosuke's face a while ago.

Kasuke staggers drunkenly onstage and falls to his knees.

HIRATA: You know where Ferreira is hiding?

KASUKE: Yes.

HIRATA: So you know where he's hiding! Tell me at once. He's in your village after all, isn't he?

KASUKE: Not in the village itself.

HIRATA: Then outside of the village?

KASUKE: You might certainly say so—but that covers a lot of ground.

HIRATA: You're drunk.

KASUKE: Yes, forgive me. I could never have come here to the bureau on my own strength. So on my way to Nagasaki I stopped for some saké.

HIRATA: Don't come so close to me. You stink. All right then, where's Ferreira?

KASUKE: If I tell you . . .

HIRATA: You'll get a large reward.

KASUKE: Besides the reward, will you let Lord Tomonaga go?

HIRATA: Yes. If you ask the bureau to save the life of Tomonaga, it'll certainly be saved.

KASUKE: Thank you. One more request.

HIRATA: Still another?

KASUKE: I ask you not to bother the farmers of the village.

HIRATA: What do you mean?

KASUKE: Not to have the farmers come to the bureau the day after tomorrow to step on the *fumi-e*.

HIRATA: All right. All right. I'll grant you that too. After all, you're all very busy in the fields. Now tell us where Ferreira is.

KASUKE: To tell the truth, I was afraid I'd be badly treated here. So I stopped off for some saké to give me courage.

HIRATA: You've already told us that.

KASUKE: I had no idea you were all so understanding here in the bureau. When I get back to my village, I'll tell them not to worry . . . that everyone here is very kind.

HIRATA: Fine, fine. Now hurry and tell us.

KASUKE: A moment ago you mentioned a reward. . . .
What kind of reward?

HIRATA: Certainly enough to pay for your saké on the
way home.

KASUKE: That's no reward. This is the first time in my life
I've ever had this much saké. I usually drink very little.
To tell you the truth, I expected to be given a rough
time here. So I stopped to drink some saké for strength.
But this is fine! I never thought you were such understanding people. When I get back to the village, I'll tell
them not to worry, that you're all fine fellows. Sir,
please tell me your name.

HIRATA: What difference does it make?

KASUKE: No, no. You must tell me. From now on, when-
ever there's any problem in the village, I know we can
call on you. Please tell me your name.

HIRATA: My name is Hirata.

KASUKE: Lord Hirata, is it? That's a nice name. Besides,
you've a very handsome and noble face. . . . What's that
sound?

HIRATA: That sound? That sound is the cry of your lord,
Tomonaga.

KASUKE: What? Lord Tomonaga's cry? Hurry. Let him go.
Hurry!

HIRATA: Are you sober now, fool? Where's Ferreira?

Kasuke, trembling, tries to speak.

HIRATA: Speak out.

> *Gennosuke enters.*

GENNOSUKE: Sir, Father Ferreira has come.

HIRATA: What? Ferreira here?

GENNOSUKE: Father Ferreira has come with Lord Tomonaga's daughter and some of the farmers. He's at the gate.

HIRATA: So he's finally come. Intending to be a martyr, no doubt.

INOUE: He's come! Ferreira has finally come! As you say, with the decision to give up his life. I want to speak with him.

HIRATA: You too, after all, are filled with the same desire as I—to defile the beautiful and befoul the noble.

INOUE: The low can see others only through their own foul spirit—and you are low. Gennosuke, bring Ferreira in. Have the others wait for a time.

KASUKE: Excuse me, please. I don't want to meet the Father. I don't want to meet the farmers. I'm quite sober now. I did a terrible thing . . . the same as Judas that Father told me about. Excuse me, let me go.

INOUE: Hirata, show this man to the door.

> *Ferreira and Gennosuke enter. Ferreira's eyes meet those of Kasuke, who is being led from the room.*

KASUKE: Father Ferreira, Father Ferreira.

> *Inoue looks at Ferreira for a time without speaking.*

INOUE: Please sit down, Father Ferreira.

FERREIRA: Thank you.

INOUE: Gennosuke, bring some cakes for Father Ferreira. Well, well, Father, you are most welcome.

FERREIRA: I've been hearing about you for a long time.

INOUE: And I've been hearing about *you* for a long time. I've been after you for a long time.

FERREIRA: I know that.

INOUE: You've come prepared to die?

FERREIRA: I don't know. If the Lord gives me the courage to die.

INOUE: But you haven't the slightest intention of renouncing your faith?

FERREIRA: Do you think you can make me?

INOUE *(laughing):* That's my job!

FERREIRA: I didn't come to Japan to apostatize. If your job is to make me give up Christ's teaching, my job is to propagate it.

INOUE: That's funny. All the Christians I ever got to apostatize said the same thing, and still they apostatized.

FERREIRA: Do you have the confidence that you can make me apostatize too?

INOUE *(laughing):* I can't say that I haven't.

FERREIRA: Will you put me to torture?

INOUE: In good time, but torture is the lowest of means. I don't want to make use of it lightly. There are those who are able to make their bodies do what they tell them, and others who are not. And so the efficacy of torture depends on the individual.

FERREIRA: Then to which group do I belong?

INOUE: *(laughing):* I don't know. That's what I'll have to find out.

FERREIRA: Do you remember the fifty priests and Christians who were martyred in Edo? They were burned to death.

INOUE: I certainly do. At the time I was in service at the Edo Castle. I remember particularly well since one of my fellow samurai, Haramondo, was a Christian and thrown in among the fifty. He was deaf to all our counsel and persuasion, and he was put into prison.

FERREIRA: Yes. Haramondo was one of the fifty. On that day the priests and the Christians were led from the prison in Kodemma, through Shimbashi and Mita, and in the evening taken to Fudanotsuji. At the place of execution stood fifty stakes, and under each stake a pile of brush. A large number of spectators were gathered. After the victims had been bound to their stakes, the executioner set fire to the brush. There was a wind that day. So the smoke and flames immediately enveloped the martyrs tied to their stakes. The first to die was a Spanish priest. Then Haramondo, lifting his arms as if he carried something in them, was next. His head fell down on his shoulders.

INOUE: You describe the scene vividly. You have a clear remembrance of it.

FERREIRA: Very clear. I had to write a detailed report of it for Rome. I also sent them an account of the Unzen martyrs. At Unzen I disguised myself as a Japanese farmer and saw everything clearly with my own eyes. It was in December of 1631. Seven priests and Christians climbed the mountain from the harbor at Kohama in the

evening. When they arrived at the top, they were lodged
there for the night, their hands and feet still bound. The
next day, the fifth of December, the torture began. They
were led to the boiling waters of Unzen. They were
shown the hissing ponds and told to renounce their
faith. When all seven refused, the officials stripped them
of their clothes, scooped up dippers of the boiling water,
and slowly poured it over them.

INOUE: Why do you go over these details? Is it to stir up
your courage?

FERREIRA: No. I just want you to realize that torture
doesn't necessarily weaken the faith of the Christians.

INOUE: Of course. I realize that. As you say, torture serves
only to make the Christians proud and fanatic. It serves
too to deepen their thoughts of Paradise. I discovered
this long ago.

FERREIRA: If you realize it, why do you still go on
torturing?

INOUE: There are many different kinds of torture. Torture
such as you have been describing, whether by fire or
boiling water, serves merely to fan the Christians' pride
and fanaticism. The suffering may be great, but they will
soon die and receive the glory of Paradise. The farmers
who watch this spectacle are also moved by the
Christians' courage. So this is the most stupid of
methods. But now, if there is a torture that does not end
in death and will last indefinitely . . . if there is a torture
that will cause the Christians to lose their pride and
make them squirm foully like worms. . . .

He laughs.

FERREIRA: You're referring to the pit?

INOUE: Exactly. Even now, Tomonaga is hanging there.

Tomonaga's groans are heard.

FERREIRA: And even he has not yet apostatized.

INOUE: Not yet, that's true. But by this evening . . . who can tell?

FERREIRA: So you won't keep your promise? . . . that you'd release him if I came to you.

INOUE: We'll release him . . . but only after you've apostatized.

FERREIRA: I've been caught in a trap.

INOUE: Of course. Just as we'd planned.

FERREIRA: Then go ahead and kill me and get it over with.

INOUE *(laughing):* That would be poor policy. I've no reason for killing you.

FERREIRA: Why do you say that?

INOUE: Father, you are what I may call the roots of the Christians. If the roots rot, then the branches and the leaves will die by themselves. You are the only priest left in all of Japan. When the farmers here in Kyushu who are still practicing Christianity in secret hear that you have apostatized, they'll lose heart and eventually apostatize too, without our having to take harsh measures. That's why I won't kill you. If I kill you, I but give you the name of martyr.

He laughs.

FERREIRA: Very well then. Hang me in the pit.

INOUE: Do you think you can stand it?

FERREIRA: I don't know. God will come to my help.

INOUE: Ha! God will only stand and watch. God is always silent. He never soils his hands. Besides, in this case, it is not my purpose to find out whether you can stand punishment or not. I'll wait for the torture to rob you of all discernment and wit and to derange your spirit. Do you understand? Through the torture of the pit, by tomorrow you'll have lost all discretion and understanding. You'll have lost your freedom to oppose my words. What I call left, you will call left. What I call right, you will call right. When I say "Apostatize," you will apostatize.

FERREIRA: You are a fiend.

INOUE: Who will win? Your God or I? Hirata!

Hirata appears.

INOUE: Please entertain Father in the pit.

> *Hirata goes offstage, leading away Ferreira. Inoue looks silently at the painting while drinking his tea. Ferreira's cry can be heard.*

CURTAIN

ACT THREE SCENE TWO

> *The scene is the same as the previous. The time is the following day.*

HIRATA: What's happened? He hasn't groaned for some time.

> *Gennosuke brings a box onstage and takes from it a* fumi-e.

HIRATA: You're not feeling well?

GENNOSUKE: I feel terrible.

HIRATA: What's the matter?

GENNOSUKE: You told me once that if I continued in this job I'd come to mistrust everything.

HIRATA: Did I? I don't remember. But to suspect every man we meet of being a thief is part of our job. Suspicion and mistrust of people eventually become part of our nature.

GENNOSUKE: I've lost all faith in everyone.

HIRATA: Even in Inoue and myself?

GENNOSUKE: Who was it that promised that when Father Ferreira would be found, Lord Tomonaga would be released from the pit?

HIRATA: Why do you ask?

GENNOSUKE: Ferreira was found, but Lord Tomonaga died in the pit this morning.

HIRATA: It couldn't be helped. When we went down to release him, he was already dead. That too is proper punishment for the stubbornness of the rebellious Christians.

GENNOSUKE: Not at all. You killed him.

HIRATA: There are things that may be said and others that had better be left unsaid.

GENNOSUKE: You've hated Lord Tomonaga for a long time. I know that. It wasn't because you suspected him in your official capacity. It was out of envy that you took such drastic revenge.

HIRATA: Perhaps you're right. Perhaps you're not. But what difference does it make? When I see that kind of hypocrite I can't stand it. I can't trust a man who is wholly intoxicated with an ideal, whether it be the ideal of a samurai or of loyalty to a person or a creed. I hate all drunks. But I don't expect you to be able to understand this feeling. And it's all right if you don't. All you need to know is that Tomonaga was a Christian, and for that reason was executed.

GENNOSUKE: I don't think that was the real reason.

HIRATA: If you keep on talking like this, you'll be suspected of being a Christian too. Hurry and lay out the *fumi-e* and call the farmers in here.

> *Hirata, laughing, leaves the room. An official enters.*

OFFICIAL: Is everything ready?

GENNOSUKE: Yes. A most unpleasant job. Won't you bring in the farmers? . . . No, first bring in Lord Tomonaga's daughter, Yuki, please.

OFFICIAL: A job is a job. There are times when we must close our eyes.

He exits.

GENNOSUKE: Everything is black, everything. Filthy. And I'm gradually becoming accustomed to the filth. That's what frightens me.

Yuki enters, followed by a guard.

GENNOSUKE *(to the guard):* Excuse me, but will you please assemble the farmers over there?

Guard leaves.

GENNOSUKE: I'm very sorry for this. You must have had a very hard day.

YUKI: Father? Where's father?

GENNOSUKE: Lord Tomonaga is safe. He must be receiving treatment for his wounds.

YUKI: Treatment for his wounds?

GENNOSUKE: No, no, nothing for you to worry about.

YUKI: I want to see him at once.

GENNOSUKE: You'll certainly be able to see him tomorrow. No need to worry about him. Instead, there's a favor I'd like to ask of you.

YUKI: A favor of me?

GENNOSUKE: Yes. In a moment they will bring out the *fumi-e* to step on.

YUKI: That's what I've been expecting. The torture.

GENNOSUKE: I beg of you, when the time comes, please value your life above everything.

YUKI: Above everything?

GENNOSUKE: Just today, close your eyes and step on the *fumi-e*. It's not in objects such as this that your faith lies. Your faith is in your heart. This carved plaque made by some nameless craftsman in Nagasaki isn't really the face of the one in whom you believe. Even if you step on it, you won't soil your soul.

> *In the meantime Hirata has entered and is listening to their conversation from a corner of the room.*

YUKI: But all the same . . .

GENNOSUKE: But all the same, what?

YUKI: But all the same, it's frightening . . . to step on a face that resembles that precious face.

GENNOSUKE: Resembles? Perhaps. But nothing more. Besides, I'm sure that even a Christian would never be punished for stepping on such a thing.

YUKI: It's not a question of punishment. But I feel I'd be defiling the one in whom I believe with all my heart.

GENNOSUKE: But if by stepping on this *fumi-e* you can continue secretly to practice your faith for a longer time, I'm sure your God would also rejoice. Isn't that true?

YUKI: If anyone else were speaking these words, I'd refuse to listen. But when you speak in this way, I don't know what to do.

GENNOSUKE: I don't know either. But I want to do whatever I can, Yuki.

YUKI: But to step on the *fumi-e* is to betray Father Ferreira and the other Christians. I can't do that.

GENNOSUKE: I forget all my embarrassment and make this plea to you. For a long time I've been in love with you. I never thought that I'd be in the position to force you to step on the dread *fumi-e*. Please step on it. Step on it and live, for my sake.

YUKI: What shall I do? I'm just an ignorant girl. In my head everything is all mixed up. Your words and the practice of my faith. Please don't say anything more.

GENNOSUKE: What is important is not form but spirit. Please consider if it isn't possible to continue to practice your faith secretly, even though you step on the *fumi-e*.

HIRATA: Gennosuke, is everything ready? Did you bring out the *fumi-e?* Oh, Yuki. Thank you for coming all the way to our bureau. You may be sure that no harm will come to you. No harm.

He laughs.

HIRATA: Bring in the farmers.

Kasuke, Mokichi, Hisaichi, other farmers, both men and women, enter.

HIRATA: Are you all set? Christianity has been severely forbidden in Japan. The edict forbidding it has been made known to all, and samurai as well as farmers are bound to its observation. You have violated this edict, not only by concealing a priest but also by continuing to follow the false religion. Formerly we should have executed you on the spot. But because of our kind regard toward you, we will give you a chance to make a new start. Those who step on this *fumi-e* will be released at once. But those who continue to disobey the edict will find that the bureau will not mollycoddle them.

Hirata takes the roll of names from the official and reads:

HIRATA: Kyosaku, farmer of Korimura.

Kyosaku steps forward, hesitates, then drops his head, unable to step on the fumi-e.

HIRATA: What's the matter? Why don't you step on it?

He hits him fiercely with his stick.

HIRATA: Next, Hisaichi.

Hisaichi stands before the fumi-e *and shakes his head; he too is fiercely hit.*

HIRATA: Next, Kasuke. Oh, it's you.

He laughs.

HIRATA: The man who has already betrayed his fellows. It's not hard for you to decide to step on it.

Kasuke hesitates, and as he is about to escape, is hit by Hirata.

HIRATA: All right. Do you want to be sent to the pit with Ferreira and Tomonaga? Your God can't be of any help now, can he?

Kasuke, his head in his hands, steps on the fumi-e.

HIRATA: Fine. This is the first man of good sense I've met here.

To the guard

HIRATA: Let this man out of the gate.

KASUKE: You're letting me go? You're letting me go? . . . In this world there are the strong and the weak. The strong, when something like this comes along, are able to take it and go to Paradise. The weak step on the *fumi-e* as I did.

> *With these cries, he is led by the guard out of the room. Even after he has gone there can be heard offstage his voice crying:*

KASUKE: Are you really letting me go? Are you really letting me go?

HIRATA: Noro . . . Noro . . . Norosaku.

NOROSAKU *(in a loud voice):* That's me.

HIRATA: What about you? Will you step on it or won't you?

NOROSAKU *(in a loud voice):* What?

HIRATA: Step on it.

NOROSAKU: On what?

HIRATA: On the face in this *fumi-e.*

NOROSAKU: Face?

> *He points to his own face.*

NOROSAKU: I can't step on my face. My feet won't reach that far.

HIRATA: Not your face. The face in the *fumi-e.*

NOROSAKU: What's a *fumi-e?*

HIRATA: Is he an idiot? Take him over there.

> *Norosaku is led out.*

HIRATA *(reading from the list):* Next, Ichimatsu. No, wait. Next, Tomonaga's daughter. Yuki, excuse me, but will you please come over here. Don't take this amiss. It's as

I told you before. This is only a matter of form. Show
that you have as much sense as this last farmer.

GENNOSUKE: Hirata . . .

HIRATA: What is it?

GENNOSUKE: Please spare her this humiliation. She's the
daughter of Lord Tomonaga, the daughter of a samurai.
And you'd have her place her foot where the farmers
have placed theirs?

HIRATA *(laughing):* That's a strange objection! A Christian
is a Christian—and a criminal. Whether he be a farmer or
the daughter of a samurai. From our point of view there
is no distinction in rank. Besides, the Christian teaching
too recognizes that all men are equal. Even if there are
distinctions in social position, there are no distinctions
of soul. Isn't that true, Yuki? Go ahead and step on it.

> *Gennosuke shrinks back. Hirata roughly
> takes Yuki's hand.*

GENNOSUKE *(his hand on his sword):* Hirata, if you treat
her rudely . . .

HIRATA: You'll slash me, will you? I overheard you a few
minutes ago, you know. I heard the advice you gave her.
Mad with love, have you become the Christians'
accomplice?

> *To the guards.*

HIRATA: Seize him. This man too is a Christian.

> *The guards hesitate and then press in on
> Gennosuke. Inoue enters with an official.*

INOUE: What's going on here? What's all the fuss?

HIRATA: I'm sorry to say that as I was having the farmers
of Korimura step on the *fumi-e,* Gennosuke tried to
interfere.

INOUE: Hirata, you've been at the bureau for a good number of years. You should know better than to stage an ugly fight between bureau officials in front of the farmers. Gennosuke's not the only one who's lost his head. Where's your common sense? We'll continue with the *fumi-e* tomorrow. Those who didn't step on it today may think better of it tomorrow. In fact, to make them think better of it is the job of the bureau. But your bullying is of no help, Hirata. Lead them away.

> *The farmers and Yuki are led away by the officials.*

INOUE: Hirata, bring Father Ferreira up from the pit.

> *The lights fade. After a few moments a spotlight centers on the three men, Ferreira, Inoue, and Hirata.*

INOUE: I'm afraid you've had quite a rough time in the pit. It must have been most painful. Hirata, put some medicine on Father's wounds.

> *Hirata does so.*

INOUE: Father Ferreira, why do you continue to endure such pain? For what purpose do you keep suffering like this? Many years ago you came to Japan from the distant southern countries, crossing the wide seas and braving many dangers. You've been in Japan for twenty years. You've buried yourself in this land without ever returning to your home country. Haven't you done enough? When you've gone this far, is there any need to go further?

> *Ferreira is silent.*

INOUE: Why do you suffer like this? What meaning is there in all this suffering? Or, let me put the question in another way: what meaning is there to this kind of life?

Do you do this for God? But, Father Ferreira, what if
this God in whom you believe is nothing more than an
illusion? Then what do you do? Does God really exist?
Is he perhaps nonexistent? If, of course, he does exist,
then there is some meaning after all in all this suffering
and in this way of life.

Changing his tone of voice.

INOUE: But if he doesn't exist, then hasn't all your
suffering, hasn't all your life so far been a kind of
madness? If this thing you call God does not really
exist. . . . Why do you remain silent, Father Ferreira?
Can't you hear what I'm saying to you? Your life till
now stands or falls on that one fact: the existence or
nonexistence of God. If he exists, then all your suffering
and hardships to this day will have a meaning. But if he
doesn't exist, then everything you've done has as little
value as a speck of dust.

Changes tone of voice.

INOUE: There is no God! Isn't that true? There is no such
thing as a God! You too, like Tomonaga, will discover
this just before you take your last breath in the pit.
You'll finally understand that there is no God, that your
whole life has been valueless, totally wasted. Hirata, take
him back. Hang him upside down in the pit once more.
Hanging upside down, Father, you can mull over God's
existence at leisure.

*The light dims and then once again centers
on the three.*

INOUE: Dawn. The sky is growing light. Father Ferreira,
this has been a long hard night for you. Did you come to
any conclusions, about what we were discussing? If God
doesn't exist, then this long torture has all been wasted,
without value. But if God really does exist, then why

does he permit us to do as we do? With these hands I have seized many Christians, made them give up their faith; and those that refused, I tortured and condemned to the pit. But in all this time God has never taken the power out of my hands. If God exists, then why doesn't he come to the help of his people? Why doesn't he raise the winds and wield the thunder and save the lives of his Christians and of you? There is no God, there is no God, there is no God! He's lost consciousness. Hirata, is there water at hand? Sprinkle a little on him. Don't give it to him to drink. If he drinks it, he'll die. Father Ferreira, have you found an answer yet? To what purpose would you continue your work in Japan any longer? To what purpose would you further endanger the lives of the Japanese? Don't think that I consider the teachings of Christ evil. I know that like the teachings of the Chinese sages, there is in them much that should be attended to. But there are two reasons why I reject Christianity: the first is that you people are too persistent in forcing your dreams upon us. Yes, far too persistent. Consider this well, Father. Were you to remain longer in the country, the ones to suffer would be the poor farmers. They are puzzled and don't know whether they should follow you or us. When you'll have gone away, they'll do as we tell them, without anxiety. But there's still another reason: that this country, no matter what lofty dreams you may have for her, is a country that will never take to Christianity. I know Japan and the Japanese better than you. There are some things that the Japanese can never achieve familiarity with, among them the Christian teachings.

HIRATA: He's saying something.

INOUE: What are you trying to say?

HIRATA *(placing his ear to Ferreira's mouth):* I can't make it out.

FERREIRA: Christ returned from the Jordan and was led
    out to the desert where for forty days he was tempted
    by the devil. During that time he had nothing to eat.

HIRATA: He's lost consciousness again.

> *The spotlight shifts to another room in
> the prison.*

GENNOSUKE: Yuki, Yuki.

> *Yuki rises and goes to the prison bars.*

YUKI: Gennosuke, it's dangerous for you to be here. If you
    should be seen by a guard. . . .

GENNOSUKE: The guard has just gone back to the guard-
    room. Besides, my good friend, Shinshiro, is on watch.
    It'll be all right for a while.

YUKI: Gennosuke, please stop troubling yourself about
    me. I don't want the same thing to happen again
    tomorrow.

GENNOSUKE: Don't worry about me. But here.

> *He hands her something.*

YUKI: What's this?

GENNOSUKE: Nothing much . . . just a covering from my
    mother and some food.

YUKI: I wish you'd give the food to my father. Is he here
    in the same prison?

GENNOSUKE *(hesitating):* Your father is well.

YUKI: Does he know that I am here?

GENNOSUKE: No. They haven't told him yet. They didn't
    want to give him further grief.

YUKI: That's right. Please don't tell him I'm here.

GENNOSUKE: I won't.

YUKI: If he should ask about me, please tell him that I'm at home waiting each day for his return.

GENNOSUKE: Yes. Oh, why must someone like you suffer in this way? Why doesn't your God help you?

YUKI: While father is suffering, it's a pleasure for me to be able to suffer with him. While the farmers are suffering, it's a pleasure for me to suffer with them.

GENNOSUKE: Ah, if only I were a Christian . . .

YUKI: What are you saying?

GENNOSUKE: I said: if only I were a Christian.

YUKI: Why do you say such things?

GENNOSUKE: If I were a Christian, they'd have thrown me into this prison with you. I'd now be experiencing the same anguish as you. If I didn't have to take care of my mother, I'd have tried to save you.

YUKI: Be careful. Someone's coming.

Hirata passes by with an official.

OFFICIAL *(looking into the room):* Everything's all right, Hirata-dono.

HIRATA: Sleep well, Yuki. Tomorrow there'll be the *fumi-e* again. The farmers had better think it over carefully. It'll be for their own good.

Hirata and the official pass on.

GENNOSUKE: Yuki?

YUKI: Yes.

GENNOSUKE: I'm sure you won't listen to me, but do as Hirata says. Tomorrow they'll bring out the *fumi-e* again. Please step on it. Please continue to live. To live is a wonderful thing.

YUKI: Your words make me very happy. But from child-hood I've been taught that the real life is not in this world but in Paradise. From Childhood this idea has steeped my heart like water. I don't know of any other way to act.

GENNOSUKE: If only you decide to go on living, there's nothing I won't do for you.

YUKI: If I weren't a Christian, I'd have wanted to live with you. Even if we'd had to live in a poor shack, I wouldn't have minded the hardship, if only I could have shared it with you. But that was only a dream that didn't come true. There's nothing more I can do about it. Please accept this crucifix.

> *She takes it from her neck and hands it to him.*

YUKI: Now please go. If you should be caught by the guard . . .

CURTAIN

The following day. The Bureau of Investi-
gation. Inoue is sitting on the mat. In the
garden Hirata, Gennosuke, a guard, Yuki,
and the farmers.

HIRATA: Now that Inoue-dono is here, the ceremony of
the *fumi-e* will begin. Yuki. You are first.

INOUE: Wait, Hirata. First, call Father Ferreira.

HIRATA: Father Ferreira?

INOUE: Yes, I have an idea.

One of the guards leaves the room.

HIRATA: Take a good look. Your Father Ferreira will be
here in a minute. You'd better display your strength of
faith to him.

The guard returns, leading the staggering
priest. The farmers, seeing him, begin to
talk among themselves.

HIRATA: Here's your priest. For two days and two nights,

like Tomonaga, he's hung in the pit, twisting his body and crying to his God for help. But this God didn't lift a single finger to help him. Not a single finger. That's the way this God acts toward you. It's up to you to step on the *fumi-e* or not. But if you refuse and are hung in the pit and like Ferreira you cry out to your God, you may be sure that he will not say a word, as if he were deaf and dumb. He'll pretend not to hear your cry.

INOUE: Father Ferreira, I'm not giving you bad advice. If you but say the word, I'll send all these farmers back to their village immediately. I won't make them step on the *fumi-e*. If the sum of Christian teaching is charity, Father Ferreira, then won't you display this charity toward these poor farmers? They are pitiful creatures who've had a very hard life. Father Ferreira, show them your love.

Ferreira is silent.

INOUE *(gently):* It must be hard for you to say that you give up your religion. To you who have come so far to spread the teaching of Christ in Japan, these words must stick in your throat. But please listen carefully to what I am saying. If you are a true Christian, you will understand that to sacrifice yourself to save the lives of these Christians is also according to the way of God. Isn't that so, Father Ferreira?

FERREIRA: My friends, who was it that promised that if I came here, Lord Tomonaga's life would be spared and that you wouldn't have to step on the *fumi-e?* And if I should now for your sake say that I give up my religion, would the bureau really keep its promise? I can't believe it.

INOUE *(sighing):* It can't be helped, Hirata.

HIRATA: Yuki, come here.

> *Yuki comes and stands in front of the* fumi-e, *her eyes downcast.*

HIRATA: Yuki, don't expect to be looked after like a child. Don't make me get nasty with you.

> *She stands there, her head hung low.*

HIRATA: Do you want the same thing to happen to you as happened to your father?

YUKI: My father?

HIRATA *(imitates her voice):* My father? Yes, your father. Do you want to die in the pit, as your father did?

> *Yuki lets out a startled cry and collapses. Hirata roughly slaps her hands. Ferreira turns about. Gennosuke tries to restrain Hirata's hand. One of the officials seizes Gennosuke.*

OFFICIAL: Gennosuke, stop it. If you don't stop, you're in danger.

HIRATA: What are you doing? Have you gone mad? No, you haven't. You've long been an accomplice of these Christians.

GENNOSUKE: Even if Yuki is a Christian, she is a helpless woman. You've been too cruel.

HIRATA: Has your pity turned into love? Do you think I'm blind, Gennosuke? You seem to have had a secret tryst with this girl in prison last night.

GENNOSUKE *(in consternation):* What are you saying? Of course I went to the prison last night. But it was only to make certain they were properly guarded.

HIRATA *(laughing):* Oh, that's most commendable. But didn't you tell her that you'd like to become a

Christian? I heard the whole conversation. Don't get
angry. I suspect everyone.

GENNOSUKE: What proof do you have?

HIRATA: Proof? What about that thing hanging around
your neck? Couldn't you call that proof?

> *Hirata has the guard pull the crucifix
> from his neck.*

INOUE: Gennosuke, you must have picked this up somewhere. You could never have done this seriously. Why
don't you explain?

HIRATA: Even if he did pick it up somewhere, to walk
about wearing objects that are under proscription is
forbidden by the edict, even to a samurai. Why don't
you answer?

> *Gennosuke remains silent.*

HIRATA: Gennosuke, since things have come to this pass,
we must consider the other officials and guards. We must
ask you to show that you are not a Christian.

GENNOSUKE: I am not a Christian.

HIRATA: If that is so, then please step on the *fumi-e*. No, I
have a better plan. If you are not the accomplice of this
Christian girl, show it by stepping on her.

GENNOSUKE: What are you saying?

HIRATA: Then you won't do it?

GENNOSUKE *(turns to Inoue for help):* Dono.

> *Inoue averts his face and remains silent.*

GENNOSUKE: Dono.

INOUE: I'd like to help you, Gennosuke. I'd like to help
you, but the officials of the bureau have their own rule.

Since you were caught wearing a proscribed crucifix around your neck, you must do as Hirata says and give proof to the other officials that you are not a Christian.

GENNOSUKE: Dono, if you tell me to step on the *fumi-e* I will do it.

> *Gennosuke makes as if to plant his foot on the* fumi-e.

YUKI *(bending over the* fumi-e*):* No, that's the one thing you must not do! Please stop! Please stop!

HIRATA: The situation gets more and more troublesome.

YUKI: Gennosuke, if you step on the *fumi-e,* the bond that binds our two hearts together will snap forever. This may have been made by an unknown craftsman in Nagasaki, but to me it has been all my life the most precious of all things. All my life I have adored it. If you step on it, you will go completely out of my life. Instead, step on me.

HIRATA: Oh, this is very interesting. I like nothing better than to throw mud at what is beautiful and spit on what is noble. This kind of perversion the officials of the bureau must all have to some degree. Gennosuke, this lady is asking you to step on her face instead of on the *fumi-e*.

YUKI: Hirata-dono, will you be satisfied if Gennosuke steps on me? Will that clear up your suspicions?

HIRATA: It most certainly will.

YUKI: Then, Gennosuke, please step on me. Everything that's happened has been my fault. Step on me.

> *She pauses as she waits for Gennosuke to step on her. But he cannot.*

YUKI: Quickly, step on me. I don't want to see you suffer.

GENNOSUKE: I don't know anything about the teaching of Christ. But now I see this clearly. If Yuki is to be hung in the pit, I want to be hung there too. If she is to be burned, I want to die with her. I want to be with her always.

HIRATA: How touching!

> *Hirata hits Gennosuke.*

FERREIRA: Stop! Stop!

> *He begins to crawl on the floor.*

FERREIRA: Aaa.

> *He twists his body and seems about to burst into tears.*

FERREIRA: You were not silent after all. I thought that you were always silent. But you weren't.

> *Ferreira stands, and, staggering, makes his way to the* fumi-e.

FERREIRA: Lord Inoue, watch carefully. Hirata, you too. I am going to step on Our Lord's face.

> *He does so.*
> *The farmers, astonished, begin to talk among themselves.*

HISAICHI: Father, what are you doing? Have you gone mad?

MOKICHI: And we were able to endure till now.

FERREIRA: Friends, I just stepped on the *fumi-e*—not as a priest, but as an individual. All of you too, go ahead and step on it. Even if you step on it, Christ won't be angry. That's what I finally came to understand. Finally. Finally.

HISAICHI: What are you saying, Father? Have you abandoned us?

MOKICHI: It was too much for him. He's lost his wits.

FERREIRA *(in a frenzy):* I have not lost my wits. I tell you in all seriousness. Christ won't be angry if you step on the *fumi-e.* He won't be angry. He won't.

HISAICHI: Father, you've become another Judas.

MOKICHI: Yes, yes, he's become a Judas.

HIRATA *(laughs)* See! Your foreign barbarian priest has stepped on the *fumi-e.* We are stronger than your God. That's what your Ferreira is teaching you.

INOUE: Stop it. Hirata, stop it.

Leaning against a pillar as if in pain.

INOUE: I never wanted to see this. I wanted to believe that you at least would conquer over me. I wanted to see by your actions that through you at least the way of Christ would sink its roots in Japan.

FERREIRA: Go ahead and step on it. Christ won't be angry with you for stepping on it. God was not silent.

INOUE *(as if in pain):* Hirata, lead Ferreira out of here. Take all the others too, all of them.

They all leave. Inoue is alone.

INOUE: Why did you have to fall, Ferreira? It wasn't only you that I was torturing. I was torturing also myself, this self that apostatized twenty years ago—and also this mudswamp of a country.

CURTAIN

A year later. The home of Ferreira, who is now known as Sawano Chuan. The shoji (sliding doors) are closed. A children's song can be heard outside. Norosaku is alone on the stage. He is shaving a large piece of wood with a hatchet. His face wears a grim expression.

HATSU *(only her voice):* Stop that. You children are devils.

CHILDREN'S VOICES *(in sing-song chant):* Fallen Father Ferreira. Fallen Father Ferreira.

Hatsu comes onstage.

HATSU: How long are you going to keep working away at that wood? You've been at it since lunch.

Norosaku, without a word, continues to move his hands mechanically.

HATSU: That sound drives me crazy.

Hatsu leaves the room. For a long time there is only Norosaku shaving his wood.

> *Then Hirata enters. Norosaku stares at him.*

HIRATA: Get out of my way, idiot.

> *Norosaku, frowning, moves backward and leaves the stage.*

HIRATA: Sawano, Sawano Chuan. Aren't you at home? Sawano.

> *The sliding doors open and Ferreira's face appears.*

FERREIRA: I'm home.

HIRATA: What were you doing?

FERREIRA: Nothing in particular. Do you want to take me to the bureau again today? Are there more articles from the Dutch ships to be identified?

HIRATA: No, that's not why I've come. Do you know what day this is?

> *Ferreira is silent.*

HIRATA: Do you pretend not to know? You know well enough. I have my perverse side, but these days you're even more warped than I.

FERREIRA: It's not perverseness. I've just lost interest in what goes on in the world.

HIRATA: As if you were dead, do you mean? I can't blame you, especially since you've shed your own name and have taken the name of an executed criminal, Sawano.

FERREIRA: I didn't take it. It was forced on me. But it no longer makes any difference.

HIRATA: Don't speak so melodramatically. You'll make
me cry. But when it comes right down to it, you're a
man of singular destiny. You came from far away
Europe to Japan, worked here as a missionary for
twenty-three years, apostatized, and are now working
for us, your former enemies. I guess you've a right to be
sad. Still, it's good to have remained alive.

FERREIRA: Do you think so?

HIRATA: It's very strange, isn't it? I was your enemy until
just a year ago, and here I'm trying to console you. I'm
something of a strange fellow too. . . . All right. If you
really don't know, I'll tell you. Today, by official order,
five of the farmers of Korimura and the daughter of
Tomonaga will be executed. Gennosuke has been added
to their number.

> *Ferreira listens silently, arms embracing
> his legs.*

HIRATA: What's the matter? Aren't you surprised, even at
this?

FERREIRA: I knew this day would come.

HIRATA: In just a few minutes the Christians, with Yuki
and Gennosuke at the fore, will be led around Nagasaki
on unsaddled horses. From Banzai-machi to Omura-
machi, to Motokonya, passing through Goto-machi to
Iwahara River.

FERREIRA: Yuki and Gennosuke? Also, Hisaichi and
Mokichi. Will they be burned?

HIRATA: No. Stakes will be planted in the inlet of Iwahara
River and they'll be bound to them. Toward evening the
sea will swallow them up little by little. Until that time,

if any of them by even a single word or gesture indicates he will give up his religion, he'll be saved.

FERREIRA: This scheme smacks of Inoue.

HIRATA: Inoue wishes to postpone the execution to the last possible moment. He is overly solicitous. And it was he who bade me come to inform you of the executions.

FERREIRA: You call that solicitude?

HIRATA: Don't judge him so harshly. To think the worst of all men is my privilege. You must have more faith in people. For example, Inoue. Incidentally, he asked me to give you this.

> *Hirata unwraps the package and pulls out a painting of Christ.*

HIRATA: Do you remember this? It's said to be a painting of Giovanni Niccolo, the Italian artist who came to Japan in the 1580's. Inoue told me to bring this to you.

FERREIRA: He asked you to bring this to me now! How cruel of him!

HIRATA: He asks that at least today you pray for Yuki and the other prisoners.

FERREIRA: Does he tell an apostatized priest to pray?

HIRATA: Don't take it so hard! The bureau has become very sophisticated in its operation. In this new atmosphere there's much that even I must still learn. The officials are now men of sensitivity. Sounds very nice, doesn't it? But I must be on my way. I must go round and make sure that everything is ready for the executions.

Hirata departs. The sound of children singing the same chant as above. Sound of falling stones. The children renew the shout: "Fallen Father Ferreira. Fallen Father Ferreira." *Father Ferreira sits, arms embracing his knees, looking up at the sky. The lights dim, indicating passage of time. When they come up again, Ferreira is still in the same position. Kasuke, dressed as a beggar, speaks to him from the shadow.*

KASUKE: Father, Father.

FERREIRA: Who is it?

KASUKE: It's me—Kasuke from Korimura.

Ferreira, surprised, closes the sliding doors.

KASUKE: Father, won't you let me in?

FERREIRA: I'm no longer "Father." The children are right: I am the fallen Father.

KASUKE: I know that. If you are the fallen Father, I am the fallen Christian.

FERREIRA: According to the Japanese proverb, those with the same disease console each other. But if you've come here to console me, there's no need for it. You mustn't be found here or you'll be under suspicion. Hurry and leave.

KASUKE: I have a favor to ask you. Won't you please open up?

FERREIRA: Why?

KASUKE: Even though you've apostatized, you still have the power to hear my confession. Please absolve me from my sins. If I stay this way, I'll go straight to hell.

FERREIRA: Go to hell? I wonder. Do you really think you and I will go to hell?

KASUKE: Ah, how I envy Hisaichi and Mokichi. Just about now they're being welcomed to heaven by Santa Maria.

FERREIRA *(opening the doors halfway):* Did you see them? Were you on the spot?

KASUKE: Yes, I was in the crowd.

FERREIRA: Tell me about it.

KASUKE: Mokichi and Hisaichi were on the third and fourth horses. The first horse was Gennosuke's, the second, Yuki's. The officials held the horses' bridles and led them from the bureau to Banzai-machi, then made a circle around Motokonya and ended up at Iwahara River. The streets were jammed with people. Occasionally one would throw a stone. Since their hands were tied behind them, they had a hard time protecting their faces. Gennosuke and Yuki were both hit, and blood gushed from Yuki's cheek.

FERREIRA: Blood from Yuki's cheek!

KASUKE: She kept her eyes down. The horse staggered and the official had to take firmer hold of the bridle. They came to the inlet of Iwahara River. On the edge of the waves they sank seven stakes and tied the seven prisoners to them. Even here the people pressed forward, shouting and laughing. There were voices crying, "Apostatize! Apostatize!"

Ferreira sighs and covers his face.

KASUKE: Evening fell and the tide came in, Father. The stakes began to sink into the water. The feet of the martyrs were now under water. Gradually the water rose to their hips. Then Hisaichi let out a loud cry which drew everyone toward him.

FERREIRA: They all came toward him?

KASUKE: Yes. Then Hisaichi began to sing:

We're on our way, we're on our way,
We're on our way to the temple of Paradise.
The temple of Paradise is far away,
The temple of Paradise is far away.
But we're on our way, we're on our way,
We're on our way to the temple of Paradise.

Father, Father, what are we to do? Father, you're an apostate too, like me. Aren't you afraid?

FERREIRA *(as if speaking to himself):* Will we really go to hell?

KASUKE: What did you say, Father?

FERREIRA: You apostatized. You stepped on the *fumi-e*. But tell me, when you set your foot down on the face of Christ, didn't you feel a pain shoot up your leg? Didn't your leg hurt you?

KASUKE: It hurt me very much.

He begins to cry.

FERREIRA: The pain of stepping upon a face that should never be stepped on.

He brings out the painting that Hirata has just given him.

FERREIRA: Is this the way Christ looked when you stepped on him?

KASUKE *(looking at it carefully, then shaking his head):* No, this wasn't the face I stepped on.

FERREIRA: This wasn't the face. Is that right? You're of the same opinion, then? The face of Christ that day was not a beautiful and noble face such as this.

> *Ferreira brings out another picture of Christ's face. It is the emaciated, exhausted face of Christ on the cross.*

KASUKE: Yes, yes, it was this face. Who painted it?

FERREIRA: I did.

KASUKE: You?

FERREIRA: To me Christ is no longer the Christ of the beautiful and noble face, but rather this Christ. Yuki that day told Gennosuke to go ahead and step on her face. Wasn't that touching? To save the man she loves, even a young girl will beg him to stamp on her. Those words were words of love. Even young lovers will sacrifice themselves for each other. Do you understand?

KASUKE: Understand what?

FERREIRA: I see that you don't. If Christ really loves us, Kasuke, then he knows our weakness. He knows how much pain you felt, he knows how we suffered in stamping on the *fumi-e*. And like Yuki that day his voice too was full of pity and tearful compassion as he whispered to us.

KASUKE: He whispered to us?

FERREIRA: Yes, yes. The Christ in the *fumi-e* bade us in tears: "Stamp on me. Stamp on me. It is for this that I exist—to be stepped on by suffering mankind, to take upon myself the pain of men's legs as they step upon me. I am in pain. But so are you. If that is so, then it's all right for you to stamp on me." This is how he spoke—just exactly as Yuki spoke.

KASUKE: It can't be. It can't be.

FERREIRA: It is. It is. It was for this that Christ shouldered his cross.

KASUKE: It can't be. It can't be.

FERREIRA: A long time ago you came to me with a problem. It was about something Christ said at the Last Supper. That night as he was seated at dinner with his twelve apostles, he turned to Judas and said: "One of you is about to betray me. Be quick on your errand." Judas rose immediately and left the room. It was already dark. Why did Christ dismiss Judas so coldly, you wanted to know.

KASUKE: Yes.

FERREIRA: Now I understand. I once thought there was hatred and anger mixed with love in those words. But as I sat here by myself in front of this painting, I came to understand that his words contained sadness and love, that he whispered them with eyes moist with love and sadness at man's weakness. He told Judas exactly what he told me: stamp, stamp on my face. Betray me. It must have been painful for Judas to betray his master. That pain Christ was better aware of than anyone else. And so he told Judas to be quick on his errand. I will carry the cross in your place. That's what he must have said.

KASUKE *(frightened by Ferreira's expression, he moves backward):* No, no, that's impossible.

> *He leaves the room as if about to burst into tears.*

FERREIRA: That's how it was. Twenty-five years I've been in Japan. It's taken me twenty-five years to learn this. I was hung in the pit, I stepped on the *fumi-e,* and I apostatized. But, Lord, I have not abandoned your face. No, instead I have found a face different from the one I knew in the past.

INOUE *(his voice only):* You're wrong. Stop deceiving yourself.

> *Ferreira, surprised, opens the sliding doors.*

FERREIRA: Who is it?

INOUE *(showing himself):* Father . . . no, you are no longer "Father." Sawano Chuan is your name now. Sawano, stop deceiving yourself. You just said that you'd never abandon the face of Christ.

> *He laughs.*

INOUE: But you've abandoned the Christians. And those Christian farmers you've abandoned have made their own decisions.

FERREIRA: Those farmers are now at last in Paradise, and Our Lord himself is binding their wounds and gently wiping from their eyes the tears they shed in this world. But my blood has also flowed. Only the Lord knows.

INOUE: In the end you were overcome by Japan, weren't you?

FERREIRA: What do you mean?

INOUE: I don't know whether you really believe what you're saying or are only trying to cover up your weakness. I don't know. But I do know that your words are not those of a Christian. They are not the words of a man who was once a priest. You may be able to deceive others, but you can't deceive me. Isn't what you are saying the very thing that the other priests branded as false?

Ferreira covers his face with his hands.

INOUE: When I was young, I put this question to one of the Fathers. In Japan, I said, we believe in the mercy of Amida. The Christians believe in the mercy of God. The mercy of Amida, we are taught in Japan, is our salvation from our weakness. We have but to cling to Amida. But the Father answered clearly: that is a different mercy from the mercy of the God of the Christians.

> *He is gradually placing more and more emphasis on his words.*

INOUE: Christian salvation is not a mere clinging to the mercy of God. The Christian must fight as hard as he can, and then his strength of spirit and the love and mercy of God come together. This is salvation. Isn't that true, Sawano?

> *Ferreira again covers his face with his hands.*

INOUE: I think that you are just bending the teachings of Christ to suit your weakness, trying to disguise your

misery even from yourself. Isn't that what is behind
your words?

Ferreira collapses.

INOUE *(speaking gently):* I can appreciate how you feel.
When it comes right down to it, it wasn't by me that you
were vanquished, but by this mudswamp called Japan.
But the swamp too has its good qualities. If you will
only give yourself over to it, you'll eventually grow
accustomed to the comfortable warmth of the swamp.
The doctrine of Christ is like a flame. Like a flame it sets
a man on fire. But the tepid warmth of Japan will
eventually nurture gentle sleep.

FERREIRA: I'm afraid I'll never experience that. I'm no
longer a Portuguese. Yet I can never become a Japanese.
I'm not a Christian, nor do I oppose the Christians. I'm
just a living corpse.

INOUE: There's only one way for that corpse to come back
to life again.

He lowers his voice.

INOUE: You must *hate*. You must hate Christianity which
has brought you to this pass.

FERREIRA: What are you proposing to me? Are you
asking me to work for you at the bureau?

INOUE: You are not Hirata. I don't ask such work from
you. All I want you to do is write. I want you to write
books against Christianity, books that will give vent to
your hatred of Christianity.

FERREIRA *(silent for a while, and then):* Is it for you that
I do this?

INOUE: You may think so. But it will also be for yourself.

FERREIRA *(in a low voice):* How far am I still to fall?

An official enters.

OFFICIAL: I bring a report on the Christians. When the sun went down, the tide came in. The stakes to which we tied them are now under water.

INOUE: Completely under water?

OFFICIAL: When I left, they were in water to their necks. Seven black heads that seemed to float on the waves.

INOUE *(as if in pain):* Were they dead?

OFFICIAL: I think they were.

FERREIRA: O Lord!

> *The sky gradually grows red. The hymn "We're on our way to Paradise" can be heard. Hirata, excited, rushes onstage.*

HIRATA: Sir.

INOUE: What's the trouble?

HIRATA: A rider has just come in from Fukuoka with a message.

INOUE: What's the message?

HIRATA: Four Christian priests have just landed in Amami O-shima. They came over in a small boat rowed by Chinese and managed to land under cover of night.

CURTAIN